FEARLESS

The Diary of an 18 Year Old
at War in the Falklands

by

Kevin J. Porter

Published by Kevin Porter

First published 2017

ISBN: 978-1546517733

Cover design and book layout: Red Pixel Creative, Waterlooville, Hants.
www.redpixelcreative.co.uk

Contents

Dedication

I have dedicated this book to Jackie my former wife who was by my side as we struggled together for 34 years and to all those who fought, and those that fell, in the war in 1982.

To my beautiful twins, Holly and Ethan who have bought so much joy and pride to my life.

Our families who supported us then and are now having to deal with us and their tragedies over these 35 years'.

I also extend my most heartfelt love and appreciation to the people of the Falklands Islands, the welcome and hospitality I have received on my visits to the Islands has been a significant part of my recovery and will never be forgotten.

Acknowledgements

I have been given the honour and privilege of being able to share the words of shipmates that I proudly served with. I would like to thank HMS Exeter RO1 (T) Trevor Ramshaw. HMS Fearless - MEM Colin Pearson, LRO(G) William Kewn, Commander John Prime (Navigating Officer) and Rear Admiral Jeremy Larken DSO (Captain) for their recollections and contributions to this book.

To Karen Murray of Oak Consulting who has painstakingly supported the edits of this work and provided valuable feedback.

To Peter Clarke at PPG Proof Reading for his professional review.

To Graham Martin at Red Pixel Creative for his excellent work in bringing this together into the format you are now reading.

Finally, to my Mum and Dad, all my family, my In - Laws - John, Margaret and Sharon Wesley and friends who have put up with me and supported me since the war. I may not always say it but their love and sometimes guidance has been a God send.

Foreword

By Rear Admiral Jeremy Larken DSO. Captain, HMS Fearless 1981-83

This is an extraordinary story, about a 100-day extraordinary war – the Falklands Campaign of 1982.

Kevin Porter was then aged 18, a bright young Tactical Radio Operator. This was mainly a 'radio-silence' war, and Kevin was handling visual signalling rather than radio nearly all the time. He was thus stationed on the Signals Bridge of HMS Fearless, and for many days at 'Action Stations' from morning twilight until darkness returned. From here he witnessed many dramatic events, and participated in lots of them. These he recorded in his diary, around which he has woven a wealth of atmospheric insight of the 'life and times' of a warship thrust, with but a few days' warning, into fierce conflict from a peacetime environment. The result is a remarkable, deeply moving - indeed an invaluable - slice of history first hand.

Kevin was part of the ships' company of an extraordinary ship. Onboard HMS Fearless the crucial landings at San Carlos Water to repossess the Falkland Islands - invaded by Argentina against the will of the inhabitants - were planned in detail, commanded and conducted. The ship was then central to the intense battle of attrition with the Argentine air forces in and around San Carlos.

Gun Direction
Platform (GDP)

Signals Bridge,
where the author
spent most
daylight hours at
Action Stations

Sea King
helicopter

Small Landing
Craft (LCVPs)

One of four
SeaCat
missile
lunchers

Sea Harrier
(landed to
refuel – an
exceptional
event)

Stern of large
landing craft
(LCU)
emerging
from dock

HMS FEARLESS docked down in San Carlos Water in her multi-role battle array. An LCU emerges from the dock; two LCVPs are on the port davits. A Sea King helicopter operates over the forecastle and a Sea Harrier refuels on the flight deck. Beneath the Bridge level are the Maritime and Amphibious (Land Force) command centres. The two black globes on the foremast house satellite communications. (Photo Capt. J P Morton CBE MN).

I cannot myself read Kevin's story without emotion. Having myself been involved in many of the same events, Kevin re-awakes vivid recollections buried deep in my memory. He and I, amongst many of our comrades, shared unique experiences which certainly changed our lives. Reading Kevin's account, it reminds me too that the nearest-and-dearest of many of us suffered indirect penalties after the war, following what we had experienced.

My personal credentials as Captain of Fearless were framed by the rather unusual fortune of being equally qualified, as a youngster, in both the surface and submarine parts of the Royal Navy. My last job as a senior submarine officer came immediately before Fearless and the Falklands affair, leading the nuclear-powered attack Submarine Squadron that included HMS Conqueror which was shortly to torpedo and sink the Argentine Navy's cruiser General Belgrano.

Whilst a veteran therefore of Cold War submarine operations, I had like Kevin no previous experience whatsoever of standing on an open bridge to be bombed and shot at by attacking aircraft protected only by a tin hat and flak jacket. This was completely novel situation!

Kevin reports that he was often very frightened. Like nearly all of us, he managed this admirably at the time. His descriptions of experiencing and controlling fear are as candid as they are illuminating. That he was not alone in this personal battle is illustrated by the record of a senior Army officer also with us:

Being on a ship whilst it is being attacked by aircraft was a completely new experience for me. You get a countdown, you can hear the roar of the engines of the jet aircraft, the whoosh of missiles firing and the cackle of small arms and machinegun fire. Then the whole aluminium and steel fabric of the ship – or cell as it seems at that moment – rocks and shakes in combination with the noise of the bombs exploding. You have no understanding of what is going on outside of your immediate area.

Kevin, whilst hugely exposed, could at least see what was going on.

I experienced fear too. Fear is however infectious, and for me it was essential above all to show no sign of such symptoms. It was helpful that as Fearless's Captain, and also the deputy and Chief Staff Officer to Commodore Michael Clapp (the Commander of the landings), I was lucky to have no time for diversive reflections. My job was to support the Commodore, confuse the opposition, position the ship best for the fight, keep my people cheerful and secure, and to bring them home safely (as you will learn, just seven did not make it). My chief enemy was prospective exhaustion that would degrade my decision making. I managed to evade this dangerous personal risk with the tireless cheerful help and support of my magnificent team, of which Kevin was one and, especially in helping me by taking charge on the Bridge during vital long hours, prominent were our Executive Officer Commander (now Commodore) John Kelly and our Navigation Officer Lieutenant Commander (now Commander) John Prime - who has also contributed to this book. To keep the ship's company and our many lodgers closely informed of everything that was going on around us, frequent broadcasts were essential. This was just one of my key tasks, which John Prime took over during actual attacks.

Kevin's record reminds me of my deep regret at not myself having maintained a diary. All I have is my cryptic Night Order Book, and for the most energetic nights there is no record at all, since I did not leave my orbit of the ship's Bridge and Gun Direction Platform. This makes Kevin's record for me the more precious. Just for a start, flooding back comes the trauma of live television beamed around the ship of our distressed families witnessing our precipitate departure from Portsmouth.

As a footnote, I'm privileged to know Kevin's West Cumbria homeland around Millom and Ulverston rather well.

Do read every page of this remarkable book; it will, in any case, captivate you.

Rear Admiral Jeremy Larken DSO
Captain, HMS Fearless 1981-83

(DSO is the Distinguished Service Order, presented to me by Her Majesty the Queen on account of the superb performance of HMS Fearless, which means of her Ship's Company, throughout the Falklands Campaign)

Prologue

These are the exact words from my diary that my Dad asked me to keep whilst I was at war in the Falkland Islands in 1982 serving on board HMS Fearless.

Dad had served with the Royal Artillery in Aden and Northern Ireland and his one regret was that he never kept a diary. He wanted me to keep this, so I could look back at what went on during those 100 hectic days in 1982.

I handed it to him when I got home but he refused to take it, telling me it was for me. He did eventually read it, and my Mum told me recently that he cried over what I had written. He still saw the small boy in me and not the fighting man that went to war. In many ways, he was right; I was very much a 'lad' when I joined HMS Fearless and it has taken many years to become the man I hoped to be.

I occasionally look at the diary, not to remind me of what happened during the Falklands War. I have that ingrained in my mind forever, but to remind me of the journey I have taken and the cost of war. It is also for my children to read when they are ready to do so.

The diary entries are all in italics and are printed word for word as I wrote them at the time. Some of the entries were written straight after air attacks and there are entries that may not be accurate according to historical records or new reports. They are the perspective and viewpoint of an 18-year-old Matelot and what we knew at the time of writing and in the heat of battle confusion often reigns. Of course, we also know how to tell a good dit! Others who were there may have a different view and I accept that. I appreciate your acceptance that this was mine aboard HMS Fearless. I have included a page from the Naval History website of Aircraft lost in the Falklands War at the end of the book – it may have different numbers to those I mentioned on the day!

As I read the diary now I note how very little emotion is attached to the words. I'm no Rupert Brook, Siegfried Sassoon or Charles Pepys; I was just a young 18-year-old Radio Operator from a very small town in Cumbria called Millom who, at the time, had not thought about the possibility of fighting a war and certainly not so soon into my naval career! To enrich what now seem rather stark observations, and to share my recovery since that time, I have added to my diary entries my current memories, feelings and emotions from each day. The actual diary entries are shown in italics throughout.

Apart from the fear and excitement of being at war, one of the things that struck me most about being in the Falklands was the similarity to the area I grew up in on the coast of Cumbria. Being anchored in San Carlos and coming 'up top' every day to see the hills on either side, reminded me very much of my childhood days in Bootle and the Fells that looked down on us where we spent so much time playing and exploring.

It was a very happy idyllic childhood, in a very quiet and safe area, where everybody knows everybody, and the children could wander for miles without a care in the world and we would all be looked out for. It was difficult for me to reconcile that happy, peaceful life with the violence that surrounded me in 'Bomb Alley'. It gave me a great sense of calm much of the time but, after the attacks, the smell of cordite, the noise, the casualty reports, burning, exploding ships, and the knowledge of death so close, also a sense of dread and fear; although if I was going to die, I took some strength from the fact that it would be in such beautiful surroundings that looked so much like my childhood home.

My reaction to the things I saw and experienced whilst at war was to have an adverse effect on my life. It took 20 years before I finally sought help for my behaviours and was diagnosed with 'Sub-clinical Post Traumatic Stress Disorder.' Sub-clinical because I could function in one way or another and I had tried hard to improve my life through education and ambition. I also had a 'nihilistic personality', which meant that I tend to self-sabotage and destroy any good things I created or that came my way. This sadly included my relationship with Jackie, my wife who I met in December 1982 on my 19th birthday. Thankfully, she would not allow it and, though angry and hurt much of the time through our early relationship and marriage, loved me and stuck by me, helping me through my troubles. Throughout all the years we remained together (thirty-four) She never gave up on me, though on more than one occasion I was ready to. We have recently, sadly, parted ways.

1

Reality Outs

I was lying on the lounge floor of my sister Kim's friends' house in Westhoughton, near Warrington, after coming back from the pub that night with her friends, watching a Star Trek film. I'd just started my Easter Leave after my first trip abroad in the Royal Navy to the West Indies and then an Arctic exercise in Norway with the Royal Marines. I was serving in HMS Fearless, the amphibious assault ship and Dartmouth Training Ship on which we trained the Royal Marines in Arctic and Amphibious Warfare and the future officers of the Royal Navy, giving them their first experience at sea and letting them know what life was really like in the Royal Navy - me too!

I was one of 'Timmington's Chosen Few', Chief Radio Supervisor Timmington, who was the Kelly Squadron training officer at HMS Mercury where all Royal Naval Communicators were trained. He had first choice of the new Radio Operators in the fleet to join him on his next draft. We were always told in training that we had to be good enough to serve with the Senior Rates if we were ever to go to war with them. This was their objective - though many probably had never been to war - that was how they chivvied us along to be the best! I passed out of HMS Mercury winning the Captain's Prize for most determined trainee – a print of HMS Kelly going into battle at Narvos in Norway during the Second World War, signed by Lord Louis Mountbatten of Burma with the inscription '…I knew and loved her from the time of her birth when her keel was laid until the keel was the last thing visible as she sank beneath the waves.' Lord Louis Mountbatten of Burma, Great Uncle to Prince Charles was trained as a Communications Officer and Kelly Squadron, where all Royal Naval Communicators were trained, was named in honour of the ship he commanded. I was chosen to join HMS Fearless as one of the best and joined the ship in South Shields where I spent several months – an education for any young Sailor!

The film finished and then news came on the telly, 'The Argentine has invaded the Falkland Islands! The Prime Minister has stated that we will be assembling a Task Force led by HMS Invincible to sail immediately to the South Atlantic to retake the Islands!' The news then went into detail about naval and military requirements.

"Kim, I better get home tomorrow, as I will be going south with the Task Force."

"Don't be daft Kevin, you won't be needed. How do you know that you'll have to go? You're too young, you won't be going."

I could hear the pleading and panic in her voice. I was her little brother, she was my 'Bibs', she had always looked out for me and cared for me. She had been my voice when I couldn't speak properly as a child and she always spoke for me. In February, she had lost her youngest son, Stephen, to cot death; she didn't need her little brother going to war only a month later.

"Kim, I'll be going. If that flotilla is sailing I will be part of it. It is what my ship does, we land Marines, and we control the amphibious war."

"But Kevin, they haven't mentioned your ship. You won't have to go. How do you know?"

"I'm a communicator, Kim; it's part of my job to know which part of the fleet belongs where, and what ships report to what Admiral! I had better get the first train home in the morning to see Mum and Dad."

The rest of the night was a blur. I think Colin, my brother-in-law and I had a few rums before bedtime. Kim woke me up at 07:30, telling me Paul - my older brother (also in the RN, but just a MUPPET - Mine Warfare) - was on the phone.

"Sprog, you best get your arse home, there's a telegram here telling you that you are on 24-hour standby to return to ship." I still don't think he realised the importance of it.

Kim and my oldest nephew Stuart (he was only 3), walked me to the local station. I had to wait hours for a train to get me to Millom, Cumbria - it is a far-flung place! I sat in a pub near the main station at Warrington mulling over the future. I checked the train times out and nipped into an Off Licence to get a few tins of 'Red Death' (McEwen's Export - beer that was issued daily in the Royal Navy, 3 cans per day, per man, perhaps replacing the 'Tot') for the long journey back to Millom.

I eventually got back to Millom about three in the afternoon. I had my blue Adidas grip, that I had brought from Jack Blair with all my belongings in for a two week leave period; a four-hour train journey from Warrington and several beers inside me and a very placid 18 year old, who had only ever had one fight in his whole life and who joined the Royal Navy because "...I didn't want to be shot at by my own people in Northern Ireland." And, according to my Dad, was not tough enough to be a Police Officer (he was being kind when he said it!). As I walked up the garden path, the front door flung open, my brother and Dad greeted me. They'd been to the 'Cons' (Conservative Club), that was obvious, and my Dad leapt on me, "This is it son, your chance to serve Queen and Country! This is what it is all about!" he pronounced, looking me squarely in the eye.

"Is it?" I snapped back as I threw my grip into the hallway. "I'm not that bothered. I'm too young to die!" It stopped my Dad dead in his tracks. There was silence, he looked horrified, stunned. His hands dropped from my shoulders, he was deflated.

Dad had served 25 years in the Royal Artillery (RA), in the best, The Kings Troop, 1st Royal Horse Artillery, various other RA regiments and active service in Aden (Married accompanied and the first time HMS Fearless and HMS Intrepid served together – I was there as well 3 years old 1966!) and in Northern Ireland with 32 Heavy Regiment, where he lost two of his Regiment. His father had served with distinction in the Royal Artillery Airborne during the Second World War getting a Mention in Dispatches and an 'In Field Promotion' rather than a Military Medal ("Bother and nonsense"). He also received a special Commendation from the South Korean Government after the Korean War and left the Army as a Major.

Mum was stoic as ever, sitting in the lounge on the sofa; though I could see she was worried and upset. I was her 'Kevin Tops', her favourite (Andrew, it's true!), there are 6 of us and she loved us all equally, still does (though Andrew, I'm still her favourite!). My youngest brother and

I have always argued this point – futile as his argument is, I sometimes let him win, because I know the truth!!

Dad disappeared upstairs, Paul and I had a few more tins and discussed what might happen and that we should go out later for a farewell pint. I had arranged to go out with friends' male and female over this leave period and had to make a few phone calls cancelling these. I spoke to Mum briefly about Dad, and she told me I should let him know what we were doing that evening. During the afternoon, the Police knocked on the door, with a telegram telling me that I had to return to ship by 07:45 Mon 5th April. I asked them if they could run me to the station at Ulverston as there were no trains running on a Sunday from Millom (still the same today) – they were unable to help! I went upstairs and told Dad I had to return to ship and also, that Paul, him and I would be going for a pint in the 'Cons', before I went on to meet some mates to say goodbye. Even now that word hurts – I knew that it really could be goodbye and I'd possibly never see any of them again. Dad looked at me from his bed and said "OK".
Just before we left for the 'Cons', Dad had not appeared, I went up to check on him and let him know we were going. He said he would meet us there in 15 minutes. It was 6 p.m.

Millom is a small town, I was well known in my early teenage years due to my outlandish 'Teddy Boy' style of dress and taste in 50s rock 'n' roll music, and now the New Romantic image. I was the only one living in the town going to war, and word soon got around that I would be sailing south. Patriotism and support was everywhere, all sorts of people wishing me good luck, young, old and people that I never really knew. It all started in the Cons. I bought 3 pints, expecting Dad to turn up. Paul and I supped ours, and left Dad's on the bar. Paul bought the next and somebody else bought a couple of 'tots' for both of us and so it went on.

Mr Guildford, my History Teacher at school was in, as usual. Mr Guildford had a torrid time as a prisoner of the Japanese during the Second World War, and was left physically horribly twisted after the torture and pain they inflicted on him. He was a great teacher and I wish I had listened to him, when he advised me I should be taking History 'O' Level – I took CSE!

"That Nott! He should go!" he said.

"Nott? The whole bloody lot should go!" I retorted.

He looked at me from his side angle that the Japanese had left him with, "Pardon? Remember where you are young man. I could have you banned from here for that!"

"I don't care, Mr Guildford. I could be dead in 6 weeks' time! This has been a cock up from start to finish. It should never have got this far."

"Well, in the circumstances, I'll overlook that remark. You be careful down there and look after yourself", he said, shaking my hand. He seemed a different man to that I'd known at school and I suddenly felt very grown up, and honoured that he should take the time to care so much after all he had been through.

Dad's pint was still sitting there. 7.30 p.m. and still no Dad, I was getting so wound up and pissed off about this. I said to Paul, "Sod it! I can't wait any longer. If he can't be arsed, then sod him! I've got to meet up with mates before I go, it might be my last chance."

For once, rather than arguing with me (he usually won most of them, he was harder), Paul shrugged his shoulders and said, "It'll be alright mate! Dad will be OK. You go and enjoy yourself. I'll let him know you waited." As an act of defiance, I necked his pint!

The night was as crazy as any that had been reported about the call up. I was the only kid in town going to war. People were so psyched up about the whole invasion, even school mates who I could never have imagined would have supported such a thing were up there, cheering, wishing me luck, "…get out there and sort the spics out!" Really getting behind me and lifting my spirits. A small town of less than 11,000 people and it seemed the whole of the past 3 years of Millom School were out there supporting me and what I was about to do. It was amazing, brilliant, out of this world. How could I have had such negative thoughts when so many people believed in what we should be doing to get the Falklands back!

There were two night clubs in the town (more like school discos, because you knew everybody up there!), and I chose to go to The Ritz with a couple of mates. I was standing at the bar, waiting to buy a round, when in walked my brother, Carol his wife, Mum and Dad. I was sodding furious! He couldn't be arsed to come out for a farewell pint with me, yet he could be bothered to go out with my 'MUPPET' of a brother who had not been called up, and have a beer with him! Mum stopped by me and hugged me. I offered them all a drink. Dad ignored me and turned his back on me. I had never been so angry and upset in all my life. I grabbed Dad by his right shoulder and swung him around. I stood in his face, my voice firm, but not loud, nose to nose. My brother tried to step in, my Mum pulled him away, telling him to leave us to get on with it. There was just the two of us. The first time I had ever stood up to my Dad, the man I worshipped. I didn't want to fight – they used to call me 'The UN' in the family because I was always the peace keeper; I stopped fights and arguments. I explained to Dad, "I was shocked, scared and not really sure how to react when the news came through. I was on my own for hours mulling it over thinking the worst. For God's sake I'm only just eighteen, I wasn't expecting this. I knew there may be a chance that I might have to go to war at some point, but the reason for joining the Navy was to keep that risk to a minimum. Now, listening to everybody, feeling the emotion, knowing how good we are; I know it's right, I know we will do the right thing and I know it is what I have to do and I am ready and trained for it. I have to go for the right reasons!"

In reality I knew I had hurt him, because he thought I was a coward with my initial views, and he had expected me to react in the same way he had reacted to the news and the opportunity I now had to 'earn the Queen's shilling'.

I think Dad was shocked that I had confronted him but maybe it was his experience as a Sergeant Major and he knew how his youngsters felt when they went into action, though he never thought he would have to deal with his own child in a situation like this, that he reacted so calmly. I could see my brother standing close by watching, in case he'd have to jump in; Mum was still holding his arm. Dad just hugged me and said, "Come on let's get pissed!" It was his way of handling these things – he was after all a 'Roughy Toughy Retired British Soldier'!

The DJ had already heard the news of me leaving, and much of the music in the club was aimed around me, Rock 'n' Roll "In The Navy", "Don't Cry for Me Argentina" and of course to end the night after many tots "Sailing", in which everybody in the club were up in a circle singing at the top of their voices. I still 'hate' this song for the right reasons, and I will be as sad when Rod dies as I will be when Maggie 'may'! (She died 2 weeks after I started this, and, yes, I was devastated – she is and will always remain my hero as a great leader – militarily and politically and a great influence on my direction in life).

The next day, was a little different; a bit more sombre.

I had arranged with one of my best mates, 'Boski', a lift to Ulverston some 15 miles away, because trains don't run from Millom after 6 p.m. on a Saturday. Ulverston was where I had to get the train to Lancaster and then London (and still do today!).

A few more pints were supped that day with Dad; I also had my niece – Claire's – christening to attend, in which I turned up in a maroon ski cardigan, dark and light blue horizontal striped T- shirt, skinny jeans, white socks and 'ballet pump' shoes, slightly late and a few beers too many!

I had to leave. I remember Mum telling my two younger brothers, Gary and Andrew, not to go far as they had to say goodbye to me before I left. They were too young to grasp the reality of the situation, 11 and 13, and had to be chased down just before I left. Dad gave me a note-book to keep a diary, as "…it was the one thing he had regretted about his active service was that he had not kept one, and he wanted me to make notes as the war went along."

The time had finally come. We had all stayed pretty strong, yet inside I was terrified that I would never see either of them again. I knew what my ship's job entailed, I'd seen D-Day Landings, I'd been on exercise and I was on the upper deck doing my job during 'air attacks', we were facing a relatively unknown force. I knew they had two Type 42 Destroyers such as Sheffield and Coventry, indeed one was built down the road at Vickers in Barrow-in-Furness, and I had been anchored not a thousand yards off the Santisma Trinidad just a year before at Portland as they were doing a 'work up' for sea and war with our Flag Officer Sea Training – the same work up as we did in the Royal Navy! I really did not fancy our chances 8,000 miles away!

I'd arranged to meet 'Boski' in the back street as I wanted minimum fuss as I left. Mum gathered the two youngest up, Tania my second oldest sister was at home, she was due to get married in June 1982, but she put her wedding off until I was back home safe. She said she couldn't get married knowing I was in danger and she wanted me at home. In fact her wedding was delayed until 23rd April 1983!

I was ready to say my goodbyes (31 years on I still break my heart at those words and now I never say goodbye to anyone).

I walked into the dining room, towards the back of the house to pick up my grip. I turned to face the gathering, seeing the tears and the pain in their faces. I wanted to stay strong, I bent down to hug my two little brothers, who were only interested in getting back out to play and I loved that because I remember that was how I used to feel at that age. Tania was next and she was sobbing her heart out, I told her to stop being stupid, then Mum who stepped forward with a little Teddy Bear, that Kim had given her that had belonged to Steven. She said, "Take this, it was Steven's. I always gave your Dad a cuddly toy to keep him safe." I couldn't hold back, we hugged for what seemed like ages, tears running down my cheeks. Eventually she pulled away and Dad leapt in, he grabbed me, physically grabbed me, so hard, it hurt. I wanted it to hurt even more, he was sobbing, no words were said, just holding and sobbing. I remember looking up into my Mum's red eyes, tears streaming down her face, I felt the pain and the terror. I could see it, see it in my own screwed up face, looking at Mum; questioning; and she was just shaking her head, she couldn't tell me what was happening to Dad, she couldn't speak, she had waved him off to war, but never her own son or seen him wave his son off to war; she looked so frightened, I could see my fear reflected in hers and Dad just kept holding on sobbing into my shoulder. I had the Teddy Bear in my hand, squeezing it so tightly as I held on to my Dad, because this may be the last time I would ever get the chance. This was when I felt most scared at leaving. I told Dad I had to leave, I pushed him away, he let go and I turned away, not looking back, walking to the door between the dining room and kitchen shutting it behind indicating I wanted no one to follow me. I walked through to the back door into the yard and stood still for 5 minutes composing myself. I didn't want anybody in the town to see me in tears. Gladly nobody chased me nor followed me outside. What had happened had happened and the next time we would see each other as a family would be when the war was over. This is how it should be, this is how it had been for generations and will be for generations to come. We are a military family!

I strolled down the back street, grip in hand, head held high, I was proud about what I was going to do - there was no one else around, except for Boski, standing beside his car. He didn't say anything, he saw my face! He waited for me to get into the passenger seat, before he got into the driver's seat. He looked over at me and said "Are you ready?" I didn't have much choice really, but Boski was a man of few words I took a deep breath and I replied "As I'll ever be."

We drove silently out of town, along the roads that we had cycled as friends with Hartley, the hills that had challenged us, the sites we had rested and camped and past the orchards we had scrumped! As we came over Grizebeck I offered Boski a tenner for petrol money, and in his own indomitable way he replied, "No Kev! You can buy me a pint (pregnant pause) if you come back!"
"Thanks a sodding bunch Boski, makes me feel so much better!" but we laughed for about 5 minutes after that, breaking the stale atmosphere and making the journey so much more bearable for both of us. Paul 'Boski' and Stuart 'Hartley' had been my best mates for 5 years and we went everywhere together (apart from the Royal Navy) and are still friends today. Boski dropped me off at Ulverston Station and the rest as they say is history!

I don't remember much of the journey on the train back to Portsmouth, but I do remember getting back on board. The ship was buzzing, it was after 22:30 – lights out - but there was no chance of that; as work was going on all over the place, and the 'leave watch' that had been expecting a quiet time – especially the ROs, were manking like hell about how much work they had had to put in that weekend to get everybody back! Not only were they dealing with the extra signal traffic about the prospective campaign, but they had to type up and send out nearly 1,000 telegrams to get everyone back on board – "Standby 72 hours' notice" and "Return to Ship". The excitement on board was immense and it was obvious this was big stuff!

The next day, I started my diary!

THIS BOOK BELONGS TO: RO1 (T) K.J. PORTER
IF FOUND PLEASE RETURN TO 3C1 MESS OR
SCYO OR SIGNAL DECK STBD SIDE OF BRIDGE

DIARY OF EVENTS AFTER BEING CALLED BACK

2

Sailing on a War Footing

Mon 5th Apr

Not a lot happened today. Turned to at 8 o'clock. All that was done was store ship, and boy did we store ship! (I think that we are going to be away for quite a while judging by the amount of stores on board). Loaded 'booties' and their weapons (you'd think we were going to invade Russia - there's that many!) and we painted the yardarms grey, but I wouldn't go up the mast - it's too high.

Secured at 5, so I went ashore at 6.30. Went to Martha's for a couple then we went to Gosport and the Belle Vue where Mai works, but she wasn't there. They had a disco on so we (me & 'Mac') went to that & trapped! Amanda (her name) was essence, she had long black hair that went halfway down her back, and she was only 16 & a half! But I didn't care, and she was well spoken, apparently well off and her father was an ex-Matelot. Then we had a Kentucky!

Everybody was involved in store ship, and we formed human chains to help get everything on board. We had so much, that we had to lay out boxes of canned stuff along the main drag, on both sides, so our head room was limited and the taller amongst us (I was 6'2") had to learn to stoop rather than banging our heads every time we walked through the ship.

It was later discovered, that the embarked Royal Marines had supplemented the reduced normal meals the chefs were serving up, by opening up some of the tins from the bottom, eating the contents of the tins and replacing the tins the right way up so that they looked intact!

The Royal Marines (Royals/Booty's) turned up armed to the teeth, and we had to find space to accommodate them and their equipment. The ship was stored for 'War footing' and we took on extra staff, 'Commodore Staff' as well as extra Radio Operators to support all the additional signal traffic and burden that was to be placed on us all as we sailed.

As we stored ship through the day, the carriers were taking on Harriers and Helicopters in the Dockyard, which would never have happened during peace time. It appeared that the gloves were off, and the norm was no more! Armaments were being loaded from the dock side and flying stations were happening in the Dockyard!

Health and Safety hadn't really hit us in the early 80s, but even we had never experienced this level of activity before as the powers that be normally had some semblance of responsibility towards the local community; that was now gone and we did what we had to do to get things done in the fastest possible time. The whole day helped create a greater sense of excitement about what we were about to embark on, and everybody worked hard together in a real team effort to make sure we were ready.

Going ashore that evening, Ian Mackay (Mac) was a good friend and we considered ourselves a little cooler than most, so avoided the rest of Portsmouth, which was packed full of Matelots, Royals, Pongos (soldiers) and others getting ready for war and full of testosterone. We decided to pop over to Lee-on-Solent for a quieter night. I knew my cousin's wife worked in a pub over there, so we hit that one. Mai wasn't there, but the disco was buzzing and Mac and I got into the swing of things. We started talking to a couple of young ladies, whom we got on very well with. Mac's friend had blonde hair and Amanda had long (half way down her back long) jet black hair. We spent the night boogying away, and outside snogging! We used the old chat up line about going to war, which seemed to work, and I was happy with how the evening turned out. I'd had far too much beer that weekend for anything else as well as having a modicum of respect for women, that I wouldn't have expected anything else (especially at that age), from them. Mac, I think, felt the same.

Tues 6th
Got shaken at 06:45 & told I had colours. Felt a little rough after night before but wasn't too bad. Did colours, went alright. Got Bridge & Ops rm ready for sea.
10:00 we sailed in Procedure Alfa rig nos 1's. TV cameras

were there. It was a noisy farewell with ships sounding their sirens at us & us returning the compliment. Dockys & Matelots lined the jetty all along the harbour to wave us goodbye, and along the hard, the ferry which came out to us fully loaded, and right out to Southsea there were people waving & cheering. Some had placards, one from some fellas on the beach said - 'GOOD LUCK LADS' and when they turned it over it said 'BOMB THE BASTARDS!' it made me feel really proud to be going. We got to Outer Spit Buoy (OSB) and dropped anchor. I was on the Fo'c'sle doing flags & it was freezing. I'd been there since we sailed and finally finished at 11:30. Went back on watch till 12:00. Had 'scran' - sausage & chips - which are being rationed out and served by the cooks. Now I'm in the mess waiting for action/emergency stations at 15:00 (only practice).

Only had emergency stations and it was wet & windy.

Got last look at England as it faded into the distance. Felt little choked. Had afternoon off.

Saw us on the News.

On watch at 08:00, just came off at 12:00! Quiet watch, but I'm absolutely shattered. We rendezvous with 5 RFAs at 01:00 - glad I won't be up - should get busy then. Saw Crichton spoke to her by light (afternoon) maybe last will see of England.

Colours is a Royal Naval ceremonial tradition in which the White Ensign and Union Jack are raised at the start of the day – 08:00. Many refer to the Union Flag as the Union Jack, but it is only the Union Jack when it is flown from the Jack Stay (flag pole at the front of Her Majesty's Warships). The role of the Radio Operator (RO) in Colours is to report to the Officer of the Watch (OOW) in full uniform in the following format:

Attach both flags (Jack and Ensign and in their bags

as they are not to touch the deck) to the appropriate 'Stay' at either end of the ship – Jack forward, Ensign aft. Semaphore Tower in the Dockyard, then raises the 'Preparatory' (Prep) pennant on the Starboard yardarm, and every ship in the yard instantly raises their Prep on their Starboard yardarms.

We have two ROs on the Ensign and one on the Jack. One of the ROs on seeing the 'Prep' hoist, comes to attention and reports to the OOW "5 minutes to Colours Sir!" the OOW acknowledges the report.
The 'Prep' is then 'jiggled' at 1 minute to Colours.
RO stands to attention "1 Minute to Colours Sir!"
OOW "Colour Party 'shun'!" The colour party comes to attention.
The 'Prep' following on from Semaphore Towers lead is lowered half way down therefore executing the signal.
RO at attention Salutes "Colours Sir!"
OOW "Pipe the Still"
The whole upper deck of the ship and Dockyard stands to attention, faces aft and salutes as the Ensign and Jack are simultaneously raised, in time with the Senior Naval Officer Afloat (SNOFA) who is indicated by a green and white pennant flying from the Inner Starboard Yardarm.
The 'Carry-On' pipe is sounded by SNOFA and the order is given to carry on and dismiss the Colour Party.

Sounds easy, but with a hangover, is a pain in the butt! When in a foreign port, this looks pretty spectacular like any ceremonial that the Royal Navy carries out and secretly I always enjoyed doing it.

We then had to prepare for sea to sail at 10:00. This entailed making sure that the bridge signal area was set up both internally and externally. The correct radio channels were activated, the signal lockers and appropriate flags (these were to prove invaluable as we sailed further south) were ready and manuals and signals were available, on the bridge and also the Operations Room underneath the bridge.

The ship was called to 'Harbour Stations' and to fall in in 'Procedure Alpha'. The whole ship's company takes part in this ceremonial departure; we are all dressed in our Number 1 Uniform and line the ship's sides as we sail out of harbour.

My 'Harbour Station' was always on the f'ocs'le to lower the Union Jack as soon as the last line was released from the dockside - the Union Flag is never flown at sea except for ceremonial occasions in sight of land or at anchor.

The last line was released and the Jack came down sharply and neatly (I always made sure it was done properly!). I fell in Port side at the start of the line with the rest of the fo'cs'le' party as the tugs pulled us away from our berth at Fountain Lake Jetty (FLJ). This is it I thought, straight into battle, there's no turning back. I truly believed that we would go to war. In fact, I had no doubt in my mind that we were going to fight and we were going to do the right thing. Mrs Thatcher was not going to back down. We do not let fascist or communist regimes take over our colonies or Commonwealth Countries and let them get away with it.

As we made our way out of Pompey, we were met with a cacophony of sound! Every ship we passed was lined, off caps and 3 cheers from each ship's company as we glided gracefully by. Every ship blasting their horn and we returning every blast back. It was incredible. The hairs all over my body were standing on end, the grin on my face was huge; none of us could believe the send-off we were getting. The whole Dockyard had turned out to wave us off. 'Dockies' and Matelots on every spare piece of jetty they could find were cheering us out. Small boats had gathered in the Harbour and escorted us, the Gosport Ferry was fully laden, people along the Hard, people in their cars sounding their horns. We sailed past HMS Vernon (now Gun Wharf Quays Outlet Shopping). HMS Dolphin on the opposite side had a full turnout of ship's company. Gosport side was chock-a-block with people waving us off. Past Old Portsmouth and the Round Tower and 'White Walls', where Nelson walked through to join HMS Victory before the Battle of Trafalgar, there were crowds of people everywhere, waving and cheering us. Indelibly scored into my mind were the four guys in white overalls on the beach with the banner "Good Luck Lads!" and they turned it around with "Bomb the Bastards!" Brilliant, just brilliant!

Anybody who didn't feel patriotic that day as we sailed, should not have been in the Royal Navy! I was standing ten feet tall with all this going on around me. The support we were receiving put me in no doubt that we were doing the right thing. I was part of history in the making. I was sailing where countless thousands of men and ships had sailed before, had received similar send offs, had created history. I was sailing in the wake of Admiral Lord Nelson, Lord Louis Mountbatten, the Victory, Royal Oak, Ark Royal and many others. This is what being in the Royal Navy was all about. If it was like this as we sailed, imagine what it would be like when we came home victorious!

Whenever we sailed, we had a following of 4 Landing Craft Utilities (LCU) and 4 Landing Craft Vehicles (LCVP), like little ducklings following mother duck, though these weren't as cute and they generally carried a nasty punch of cargo and men! They belonged in our tank deck (LCUs) and hanging on davits on the port and starboard side (LCVPs). We always went to anchor just before going into harbour to drop them off and always on our way out to pick up our precious babies. We had to come to anchor to lower our stern gate, flood the tank deck dock and bring the babies in.

Captain Larken loved naval tradition, and always insisted that with the Cable party, a 'Bunting' (RO Tactical) was present to use 'Cable Flags'. These are a numeric group of flags on 3ft long wooden poles that were raised to indicate how many cables of the anchor chain had been lowered or raised whilst anchoring or weighing anchor. If we were anchoring at night, I would use a 3 inch signal lantern with a red filter over it and send the number to the bridge in Morse code. Of course being the sprog (baby) of the department, it was my task to do the Cable Flags. I had been on the fo'c'sle since 09:30 and it wasn't the warmest of days. Captain Larken's passion for tradition, and the use of signal flags for silent signalling was to prove a godsend and also kept the Tactical department very busy during our trip south.

When eventually I did finish my watch, I was able to grab some 'scran' of sausage and chips. This was being dished out by the ship's cooks (we didn't have chefs in the RN they weren't good enough!). I lie; these guys worked miracles with what they had to feed an extended ship's company of around 1,250 men. The Chefs generally fed a crew of 600 in normal circumstances. We had 1,250 men almost daily onboard until the day of the surrender. For the landings we had 2,000 men on board. Generally, we were able to help ourselves at the serving counter, but nobody knew how long we were going to be at sea, so the chefs were rationing the portions. No matter what, any food was good to have!

I then went down to the mess, waiting for exercise Action Stations, as part of the start to work up to war. It had been a hectic and emotional morning, so a couple of hours of peace and quiet was a welcome break. When the time came, it was only a "Hands to Emergency Stations", not as serious as Action Stations, but important nevertheless as we had to know where we needed to be if we had to abandon ship.

During this time, my emergency station was like my action station; on the Starboard bridge wing. We saw a ship in the distance and I challenged the ship by Morse flashing light to identify itself, using a NATO recognised format. The ship identified itself as HMS Crichton, a Ton Class Mine Warfare vessel on which my older brother Paul had served in the early part of his naval career. We exchanged pleasantries and in accordance with Royal Naval Protocol, Crichton requested permission to proceed as previously directed (being the Junior Command), which of course we granted.

The weather was dull and grey, but this did not stop me from sitting on the upper scupper after we secured from emergency stations. The ship may be crowded, but there is always time and a space to be alone. I grabbed a cup of tea in my blue plastic 'action mug' and wandered off on to the flight deck. I sat on one of the aft Starboard bollards on the flight deck, watching the white cliffs of the Isle of Wight disappear into the distance. The clouds were low, and visibility was poor.

I felt very emotional at this point and sobbed for a minute or two as I watched the cliffs disappear into the distance. I really did think that this was the last time that I would see England.

When I made my way back to the mess deck, I was feeling pretty low. I had a couple of hours off before going back on watch at 20:00. We watched our departure on the news which again bought a lump to the throat. I hoped to catch an hour's kip, but there was too much going on, and I was back on watch.

As signalmen it was our job to look out for ships or threats in the distance. We were due to join up with several Royal Naval Auxiliary Vessels - Galahad, Tristram, Geraint and various others to support us in our landings and our journey south. My diary was carried in my respirator bag in a waterproof bag wherever I went. If the ship was to go down, I wanted this diary with me. I originally kept a record of all ships that joined and on what time and date as we sailed south, but deleted, ripped out and shredded the pages as we entered the TEZ, just in case I got caught as a POW at an early stage, and the enemy then had a record of the whole Task Force! Whether this was naivety on my part or over cautious being a communicator I don't really know, but I wished I'd kept that list and the dates. With each ship spotted, we had to exchange IDs visually using flashing light and I was so glad that I was not on watch from midnight: -

1) Because I was knackered from being awake from such an early hour and the emotion of the day, especially seeing Crichton and the Isle of Wight disappearing.

2) Somebody else needed to take some flak and let me take a break!

It was going to be an extremely busy watch for someone and it wasn't going to be me this time. I really was shattered, emotionally drained and felt the need to 'bash some Zs'.

3

A Life on the Ocean Wave

Wed 7th

NOTHING HAPPENING! So I will discontinue writing (to save paper) until something does eventually happen. Had 'roughers' (force 8), felt grotty but wasn't 'huey'! Was alright in the afternoon.

What this means is that there was a strong wind, the sea was rough, with waves breaking over the bough. HMS Fearless, being a flat bottomed ship, lurched and rolled a lot in heavy weather. Much to the merriment of the 'Old Sea Dogs' on board, many of the crew suffered from sea sickness - huey - due to the motion of the ship.

If you have never been to sea or suffered from sea sickness, it is one of the most awful feelings ever! Your head aches – especially sinuses - your stomach is constantly moving and cramping. The best cure is to stay in your pit and see it through. This isn't always possible and the brown, waxed inner gash bags we had on ships in those days were very useful in keeping areas clean in rough weather.

Thur 8th

Saw a Whale today! The first I've ever seen living wild &

free! Two more ships joined.

Being in the Royal Navy, I tended to take many things that we did or saw for granted. As we sailed further south, seeing whales and other such creatures became a regular occurrence. I was particularly impressed with the first one though. To see it 'blow' and surface really was beautiful; they are majestic creatures.

Some people will never ever see a whale in the wild in their life time but for me it became normal. This didn't really hit home until some 30 years later when I was on a Cruise through the Norwegian Fjords with Jackie and the children. I had been there and done that, but they still took my breath away as we sailed close under the vertical cliffs, the clear air and beautiful sunsets at 23:00. Jackie and I had just finished a late dinner and as we walked around the deck that evening she said to me she would love to see a whale. I said I'd keep a look out for her, we were bound to see one this far north. As I was leaning over the guard rail that evening, listening to the soothing sound of the sea pushing away from the hull and just scanning the horizon (some things never leave you) I caught sight of something about 500 yards out, something breaking the surface. "Jackie quick – there's a whale!"

I pointed in the direction that I had seen it; I never took my eyes of the area and within seconds it surfaced again and blew! Perfect timing! That whale sighting helped make her cruise even more special.

Fri 9th
Quiet! Cleaned up for Captain's rounds. Another ship joined.

Sat 10th

Not a lot happened today. Yeoman had words with me about my attitude towards the LRO (T). So I told him why it was, so he got him too & all of a sudden his attitude towards me changed (better!). Went out in the sea boat to collect an airdrop from a Nimrod (News & Videos).

As you can imagine, individual's thoughts and tensions were fairly high on board. Some were gung-ho, others quiet and others couldn't help taking their feelings out on other people. Greg, my Leading Radio Operator, was one of them. Since we sailed he had been constantly digging at me, making snide remarks and pushing me around. Today we would call it bullying. He was much older than me and in a position of responsibility and the person who I reported into. I didn't really like him much, but respected his position and worked as hard as I could to make sure I was good at my job and not to upset him.

On this day, I just snapped back at him. I can't remember what was said, but it was done on the bridge in front of the OOW and others up there. I took my headphones off, and stormed off the bridge, getting someone else to take over. I was raging and on the verge of tears. One of the other ROs passed the word to the Yeoman that this had happened.

Yeoman Moutter appeared on the bridge wing looking for me. He too started to give me a rollicking and I let him go on. I then let rip about everything that had happened from when we had sailed. It wasn't just on watch, but we shared the same mess and it continued in there. He was a thoroughly horrible individual in my eyes. I was given a reason for his acting like he did, from the Yeoman, and as far as I was concerned that was not my problem. It must have been difficult for him, but he shouldn't be taking it out on me; we all had our worries and concerns to deal with and as far as I was concerned we should be supporting each other especially the senior members of the department looking out for the younger ones. The Yeoman took all this in and to be fair to him (I didn't always have a good word for him at the time), he also took Greg to one side and had a discussion with him.

This had the desired effect and the change in Greg was almost instant. There were no more problems between me and him for the whole war and he became very supportive.

Whenever the sea boat was sent away, there always had to be an RO on board to keep in contact with the ship. It was a task I loved doing. A small whaler, in the middle of a gigantic ocean miles away from the ship. I don't know if it was the risk factor or the being at one with nature, but it was always a great experience (well almost always!).

The task we were sent to do on most occasions whilst away was to pick up mail from other ships and deliver parts or people. Having an airdrop of mail and stores from a Nimrod was something we had done before. We had to locate the containers quickly and haul them on board the sea boat to get back with the goods. Mail was always a great morale booster, so it was an important task to get right; if you messed up with the mail, you would be in deep doo with your shipmates!

4

Half Way There

Thurs 15th

Long space! Nothing much has happened till now. Crossed Equator at 20:47z.

This was a first for me! Up to now, our trips had been to the 'WIndies' and Norway. Although as a child I travelled extensively with the Army and had spent time in Aden during the Uprising, I was only 2 or 3 years old. When I said earlier I took a lot of things for granted this really was something special to me. I don't know why, it just felt important. We had crossed into the other half of the world and were now closer to the war zone!

Fri 16th

Had 'Crossing The Line Ceremony' at 0800z. Got nabbed & ducked, thus being initiated at King Neptune's court. Looking forward to one on way back!

Many years later, Commodore Michael Clapp and Major Ewan Southby-Tailyour wrote a book 'AMPHIBIOUS ASSAULT FALKLANDS – The Battle of San Carlos Water'. The book, like HMS Fearless', motto was "As in the Name" and tells the story of the amphibious operation to retake the Falkland Islands. On this day in 1982, they describe how Sandy Woodward turned up unannounced on the Fearless (they were informed that two helicopters were on their way): Here is their account:

"…and out he stepped… We were not, however, prepared for what was to take place. Although he was Senior, we had not expected Sandy to want to take the lead at this meeting in such a forceful and tactless way. We believed that we were the best people to discuss amphibious problems and expected him to want to hear our views. Instead he gave us a number of instructions which we considered to be complete red herrings. Finally, Sandy instructed us to consider another and even more alarming idea he had. He said he was considering a 'feint' lasting two or three days using Fearless, Fort Austin and Resource as well as some LSLs. This required me to disembark some of my staff (and some of Julian's) to a destroyer, while Fearless' group, acting as decoys, would close the Argentine coast in order to draw the Argentinian Air Force so that we could initiate an air battle. At the same time the two staffs would be closer to the Falklands coast in the destroyer 'making amphibious noises over the radio' simulating an assault. This raised two obvious concerns: one was the safety of Fearless herself – we only had one ship capable of commanding a landing – and the other was that both my and Julian's Task Group would be left leaderless. All this was seen on board Fearless as an unnecessary attempt to dominate and it acutely embarrassed the naval members of my staff, while infuriating the Royal Marines and, more particularly the Army members who were new to the Royal Navy and its quirks. Trust was broken and it would take a long time to repair.

Without much firm direction from home, but with some

ill-conceived ideas from our co-CTG, we in the amphibious flagship were getting on with it. We badly wanted to meet our Task Force Commander, the CinCFleet."

Even at an early age, I understood there would be a level of politics at the top, but I was shocked and horrified to read the above. I had always heard that the Admiral was perhaps not the most popular of senior figures in the fleet, but his apparent ignorance of amphibiousity and the contempt with which he treated his own senior officers in this instance is beyond compare! In my view, a good leader should always listen and utilise the skills around them to ensure they achieve success and this account spoke volumes!

There are however other views on this meeting and on Admiral Sandy Woodward himself. First impressions always count and these were my initial views. I have had the privilege of communicating with our Captain Jeremy Larken during the final stages of this work, and he has very kindly provided some illuminating insights into Sandy Woodward, and has given permission for me to share some of this. A key document shared is from Jeremy's contribution to an 'Emergency Services Incident Command Manual called 'Tales from the Hot Seat', edited by Prof Rhona Flin (Aberdeen University) and Kevin Arbuthnot (A Senior Fire Office West Yorkshire Fire Rescue Service)' 2000:

"The senior commander afloat was Rear Admiral Sandy Woodward. The situation was however complicated by a command structure under Admiral Fieldhouse which appointed Sandy Woodward, Michael Clapp and Julian Thomson as co-equal Task Group Commanders, each Task Group having of course a particular function. Sandy

Woodward had degrees of primus inter pares status which varied and were by no means always clear to those concerned. Notwithstanding Admiral Fieldhouse's superb personal leadership of the campaign from his shore headquarters at Northwood, Middlesex, the consequent misunderstandings were serious. To ensure an absolutely unambiguous command and control structure is a lesson of war clear to Alexander the Great, Marlborough, Napoleon, Nelson, Wellington, and the great German Army commanders alike. Such difficulties apart, it was a shining feature of the Falklands Campaign that overall we proved so ready and so flexible, and that really very few ancient lessons were forgotten.

Having served Sandy Woodward four times, I knew him well with awesome admiration - and deep affection - as an intellectual, keenly astute and a masterful submariner by background. The Rt. Hon Margaret Thatcher in 1992 wrote:

There were those who considered him the cleverest man in the Navy. .... He was precisely the right man to fight the world's first computer war.

His agile brain generated bright ideas at an alarming rate. At inception these were generally not ordered, and his hapless staff could readily be run ragged without stern prioritising by a firm deputy – which it had once been my privilege to be. Michael Clapp knew Sandy Woodward only slightly and Julian Thompson not at all.

A meeting of these seagoing principals would almost certainly occur near Ascension Island where the small Carrier Group had assembled before us. Sure enough, as soon as FEARLESS was within range, a helicopter bearing the Admiral approached. The pressures from the Commander-in-Chief's headquarters at Northwood were already acute and there was a residual air of stress aggravated already by the ambiguities in the command structure. Some days before, I had decided to attempt to prepare my leaders for the type of intercourse such a meeting was liable to bring. I was anxious above all that they should recognise the inevitable barrage of Woodward ideas, some projected simply as a cheerful agenda for lateral-thinking debate. They should stand their ground, especially on amphibious principles – on which the Admiral would wish to be educated.

Everything turned out as predicted, but my attempts to fix the chemistry proved in vain. My two champions were defensive, and dismayed and offended by Sandy Woodward's breezy and provocatively creative demeanour. This set a pattern of mistrust, almost adversarial, between the offshore Carrier Group and the inshore Amphibious Group - the two principal headquarters groups afloat. They rubbed along together. But it was a sadly raw relationship, fraught with misunderstanding and perceived offence. I did go on trying to moderate these stresses and strains, with some modest success. Max Hastings and Ewen Southby-Tailyour, in books about the campaign, were amongst those who had kindly things to say in this respect. Max Hastings, in my view, the most outstanding of a strong media corps present in the South Atlantic, wrote with Simon Jenkins a book (1983) which remains one of the most powerful accounts of the campaign amongst a great deal of more-recent literature. It was there with gratitude that I read that:

Larken ...... was to play an important role in keeping 'combined operations' combined. His ..... great skill in sympathising with other men's points of view contributed enormously to the eventual success of the amphibious operations.

Clear Lower Deck

Sandy Woodward, also decided to do the motivational speech to inspire us for the fight to come. We had cleared the lower deck and were gathered in the Tank Deck amongst the tanks, weapons, ammunition and men of war, the Royals, and Pongos. We were called to attention as he stepped through the hatch into the Tank Deck. He took his place on the boxes of ammo so he stood above us. He started speaking. I cannot remember all he said but I do remember the words "…take a look at the man either side of you, your friend, shipmate or comrade. You may never see them again after tomorrow." In terms of inspiration and motivation this was both ineffective and even damaging to the men listening to him. I really despised him for those words. I was scared enough but also nervous, excited and raring to go, and suddenly 'fwoof' with those few words, he had brought me down to earth with a crashing thud. I looked at Bill sitting to my left and he looked at me, we both said together 'Wanker'. Reflecting now my most charitable thoughts are that he was trying to bring reality to the situation but, in reality, all he did was heighten the fear that already threatened to overwhelm me at times. I didn't want to lose anybody, let alone Bill Byrne!

Jeremy Larken in sharing his views with me wrote 'Sandy was a man of exceptional intelligence. Not least amongst gifted people, human relations were not his strong point.

His ability for instance to empathise with a ship's company was lamentable, least of all on 'clear lower deck.'"

One could argue that Sandy was out of touch with the thoughts of his men and we were his men under his command; though having studied Leadership and Coaching in my later life, I can fully relate to the words that Jeremy has used regarding the late Sandy Woodward, and recognise that my early thoughts also came from a level of immaturity as part of my growing up. I also believe that having to do the rounds of such an immense task force could not have been easy for him, knowing that he had ultimate responsibility for sending these men into battle and sadly their deaths.

Sat 17th

Anchored at 0800z at Ascension Island. Got relieved late so I was on watch from 0400 to 0810 - not impressed! Did Jack & Cable Flags. Saw some sharks, 1 hammer head & one ordinary looking one. Stacks of Black Sea Piranha type thingies that will eat anything. Was looking forward to hands to bathe!

The waters around Ascension Island were amazing. The colour of the sea was a pure aqua marine, clear and clean. You could see down so deep. The water was teeming with sea life including schools of Hammerhead sharks. It was like watching a Davidttenborough documentary. Wherever you looked there were fish of one type or another.

It was the first time I'd seen a Hammerhead shark and they really do look weird. Later, during our time at Ascension, we saw a school of twenty or more swimming around; it was a beautiful sight and something very few people get the opportunity to see.

One of the other exciting fish around Ascension was tough black piranha (Parrot) type fish. They would leap on anything that was thrown into the water. Throw a bit of bacon in and the sea looked like it was boiling as the fish attacked it!

The Chinese Laundry that remained on board loved them. They were easy to catch and could be traded in with the 'Dhobi Wallers' for a couple of tinnies. A few of the lads always had fishing gear on board. There was plenty of exotic fish being caught and cooked fresh for scran by the chefs. I also got my first taste of shark during this time; several were caught and served up for dinner. It was delicious!

This was now to become a period of waiting for us. Waiting for other ships, waiting for diplomacy, waiting for news if we were going or not. It was never really boring because there was so much going on. There were ships joining on a daily basis and we had thousands of signals to deal with in the MCO or up top on the bridge; we had ship and aircraft recognition training and constant training for Action Stations and emergency stations.

As the various STUFT ships arrived, we had to exchange IDs with them. Most had a naval contingent on board and were pretty good at responding, but some were painfully slow, and I often wondered if we were ever going to fire a shot across their bows as they got closer to the anchorage! There were times that the OOW did nothing about our reports of ship sighting as we shall discover in a few days' time!

Throughout this time there were flying stations with stores and people moving around the various ships and to 'Wideawake' Airport on the Island. I think the 'Yanks' called it Wideawake as a joke because they were so slow answering our radio transmissions, sometimes taking as long as 15 minutes to respond in the early days of the anchorage.

5

The Long Wait

Sun 18th
Still anchored. Had bit of panic stns. Submarine detected, believed to be Russian. All set to move off. Ops Rm wasn't ready. CCY not impressed! All 'Bunts' got rollicking of him. He doesn't think we know we are at war! **Hermes, Invincible** *& others with the other Task Group thinned out.*

All the ships and crew were at a much-heightened state already. Some were jittery and reacted to the slightest thing. Sonar alerts were quiet often eventually defined as whales or just rocky features on unchartered waters but we weren't taking any chances!

We weren't aware of any submarines due in the area, but this was a confirmed contact. We could only put it down to the Russians, as we knew most of the NATO movements and the Argentines didn't have the capability to travel this far. I don't know if it was a little bit of complacency on the 'Buntings' part or just not knowing who was responsible for what, but when we were called to Action Stations on discovering the sub, the CCY got into the Ops room only to discover the books and call signs, formations and other things that should be set up at a Radio Operator station were not done. He went ballistic! I don't know who was responsible for setting the Operations Room up, but I certainly wasn't detailed off to do it and there are were a lot more senior comms ratings than me to know what they were doing. I was usually detailed off to scrub the bridge wings, or paint this or that. It didn't worry me because it meant I was up top, getting the sun and sending or responding to flashing light signals – I really loved this part of the job.

I did feel hacked off that the Chief doubted our commitment to the task and what we were preparing for. We all worked hard as a team, and made sure we were the best. This was a slip up and it never happened again. I think that the Killick of the watch should have had the accountability for this, and made it part of the handover process. Whatever the reason it didn't happen but after this we were always ready.

The Command structure was such that the Carriers were part of one Task Group and we were part of another but we were all part of the same Task Force. As soon as the sub was detected, the Carrier group upped anchor and went off to sea with their protection force. By moving around and adopting zig-zag formations, this meant that the ships never stayed on a steady course, and moved either by timing or by a visual signal order so they were more difficult to attack by torpedo. We stayed where we were!

The fact that we stayed at anchor, also gave us an indication of what the senior CTG thought of the amphibious units – I think he wanted to prove he could do the landings with his own carriers and helo force and not need us!

Mon 19th

LSLs rejoined us, making up our Task Group. Still anchored!
Tragedy struck. My beautiful tan has started peeling. Aaarggh!
Gone day worker from 2000z. Bill Byrne upset 'coz not got a mention yet! So decided to mention him.
Got another 'maily' from Kim. Got 1 yesterday & 1 from Dad. Great news from Kim, cheered me up no end! Morale on board still high, but mail is now censored. Lads a bit dischuffed!

The LSLs Sir Galahad, Sir Tristram, Sir Geraint, Sir Lancelot, Sir Belvedere finally caught up with us. We generally could only make about 20 knots top speed, but the LSLs were even slower travelling at only 12 knots. These ships were Landing Ships Logistics but under the RFA Flag, so commanded and manned by Merchant Navy with Army contingents. They were part of our Task Group and we were nearly a complete Amphibious Group, but one major unit was missing: HMS Intrepid. She was our sister ship and the two LPDs did 3-years-on 3-years-off as Dartmouth Training Ship (DTS) and the amphibious role with the Royal Marines. Each ship took a break to go into refit for maintenance after their stint.

Most of the older blokes on board had served on both; it seemed that if you had been on one, then you were destined at some point in your naval career to go on the other. There was still a lot of intership rivalry between us, but generally it was good fun.

During the summer, I always tend to go very brown, and in prolonged periods in tropical sunshine it can be difficult to tell what race I am just by looking at me! During my travels, I have been mistaken as a long lost member of an Arab Tribe in Sharjah (got a great deal on a gold necklace though!), Italian, Spanish, Pakistan and to top it all off, I was in Ritzy's in Portsmouth one night and a group of Arab Naval Officers that were visiting, approached me and started asking me questions in Arabic! Abroad, I could cope with; but in my home port?

Rarely did I peel and rarely did I use sunscreen. Far from it, baby oil or vegetable oil with carrot juice was our preferred method of 'bronzing', with liberal amounts of chilled baby oil rubbed into the body as after sun! It generally worked, but I had not been so close to the Equator as we were now, and even though I didn't go red, I obviously burnt at some stage and my tan started peeling. I was horrified! Not sure why, because we weren't going to be in contact with any females for a while!

As we were 'reasonably' quiet at anchor, the CCY decided to put in a relaxed watch keeping system. This meant that he needed some people to work 9 - 5 as general dogsbodies and I was one of them. Whilst the other lads got to deal with signal traffic, those of us on days were scrubbing, painting, sewing flags and generally doing what we were told to do. It seemed like a good scheme as we would get all night in for a while, until of course there were little things like refuelling or store ship (RAS) to do late at night! I think this system lasted a whole 4 days before being back to normal.

Bill Byrne had become one of my best mates since the time we were at Mercury together. We were in the same class and we used to practice our Morse together, ensuring we got through the test at the end and successfully passed out. On our passing out parade my parents were late to arrive due to mishaps with the car they were driving. In fact they were so late they didn't actually see me pass out or receive the Captain's Prize for the 'Hardest working and most determined student!' Bill's Mum and Dad and his sister Melanie took me under their wing until my parents arrived. Bill and I became very close, and our first 3 drafts together were SBS Chatham May 1981, HMS Fearless in South Shields September 1981 and Northwood NATO Command Communication Centre August 1983.

Bill was slightly older than me and I thought he was very cool. He taught me to dance (just relax, move your feet and get into it), introduced me to Jazz Funk and his own way of chatting up the ladies - he was quite good at it! We also got into trouble together!

The first time was whilst at SBS Chatham in July 1981 3 days before the wedding of Prince Charles and Lady Diana Spencer. Bill and I had been to the Pembroke 'Bop' and had a few too many to drink. We had our own cabin at HMS Pembroke and somebody forgot to set the alarm clock! We were about 20 minutes adrift for duty, and reported to the Leading Reg. He gave us a bollocking and we apologised, but we still had to see the Joss Man. The Killick Reg told us to "be remorseful and apologise, we're quite relaxed down here, so long as you apologise to the Joss you should get away with a bollocking and a bit of running around for him." We were really grateful for this advice and fairly relieved. What I couldn't control however, was my nervous smile that came across my face every time I was being told off! I didn't even know I was doing it half the time, but the person giving me the bollocking thought I was taking the mick; as did the Joss! He actually told us both, "...that he was going to let us off this time, but because Porter thinks it is so funny, you will report to Commander's Table at 08:00 next day!" I tried to explain and apologise, but he was having none of it. Bill was furious.

Next day we went in front of the Commander and received 5 Days Number 9 Punishment - 5 days extra duties (spud bashing, sweeping leaves and confined to barracks) which meant that our plans to go 'Up Town, in Rig for the Royal Wedding' were well and truly scuppered! We were the only two non-duty crew left on board that day, and to top it all off, Bill got turned into sick bay the day after the table with flu and didn't do any of his punishment - I was on my own!

When we joined the Fearless in South Shields, we joined as a whole ship's company in a mass troop movement. The Navy had requisitioned a train and 500 Matelots and bootys travelled from London to Newcastle together - an interesting journey!

On our first night in South Shields, the CCY had organised a piss up for us all to get to know each other. The details were published and RV point was established. Bill being Bill was not going to turn up on time, as it was 'fashionable to be late'! What choice did I have but to follow and support him? We turned up at the pub having had a few on the way, to be greeted by the rest of the Comms department including the Senior Communications Officer Lt Cdr Bill Whelan. He was sat at the bar lording it up and we were introduced:

> SCO "Hello, I'm Lt Cdr Bill Whelan. But you can call me Sir!"
> "Evening SCO, I'm RO Byrne and you can call me

RO Byrne!"
I just wanted the ground to open up and swallow me! Bill just didn't care!

Our next scrape came later in 1982 when we were in Venice. We didn't tend to go ashore to all the Matelot traps, and liked to experience the proper local culture and go around the back streets of the towns we visited. On this occasion, we were really having a cultural trip. Sadly, Bill's sister Melanie, fiancé had been killed in a vehicle accident a few weeks earlier. We were away, but Bill woke up one morning really agitated, saying that he had dreamt that Mel was calling him and she was very upset. Later that day he got a telegram informing him of the accident. Bill was a Catholic, his father was an Irish Scouse and a great bloke; they really did look out for me. Bill wanted to go into a church, light a candle and say a prayer to pay his respect. I was fascinated by this and asked him why Catholics did this. He explained it to me and I was truly moved by his emotions.

We then proceeded into deepest darkest Venice, and found a nice family pizzeria that had a few old locals in eating and drinking. Neither of us could speak Italian, but we managed to order some fantastic pizza and garlic bread with jugs of wine. We spent some time in there. I know this, because we had two empty jugs of wine that had been filled more than once and the proprietor had shut up shop and left us in there alone with our wine and whatever snacks we had at the time. We had drunk a few jugs by this time, and decided it was time to leave. We knocked on the counter to try to attract somebody's attention so we could pay and also called out through the door; no one came. We did what any honest, drunken sailor would do. No, not do a runner, but left a few Lira on the counter (probably not enough, but it made us feel good!) and walked out shutting the door behind us!

Up to this point we had been in great form. Afternoon wine and fresh air is a great recipe for disaster especially if one of you is feeling a bit maudlin! Bill suddenly started having a go at me for taking the mickey out of him for lighting the candle. I tried to explain that I was genuinely interested and very moved by what he had done. It didn't help to calm him down, instead it made him worse. He started shouting and pushing me, and we were like two school boys, "You hit me first", "No! You hit me first" as if trying to protect ourselves if we got caught and then blame the other for starting the fight. In the end, I swung out and hit Bill, he hit me back and I hit him again, catching him bang on the nose, which immediately started bleeding, and he started crying, then I started crying for hurting him and we were standing on this little bridge over a canal in Venice crying and hugging each other because we'd hurt each other. I think a lot of this was also part of the crap we had gone through in the Falklands coming out. We sorted ourselves out and I realised my white shirt was covered in blood.

"Bloody hell, Bill! How are we going to explain this?" more tears! He then gave me his cardigan (yes we wore cardigans) to cover most of it up, but there was plenty of blood still visible. It was decided that Bill had fallen up some stairs and I had to pick him up, which is how the blood came to be on my shirt. We got away with it! This was the first and only 'fight' I had during my naval career. It didn't affect our friendship at the time though, sadly, it did later on in the year!

Whilst at anchor, mail was coming on board fairly regularly

and with this came an outbreak of morale. I was getting letters from all members of the family separately, as well as from people in Millom wishing me well. Kim's letter contained the fantastic news that she was once again pregnant with my now nephew Peter. After the dramatic events of February, this was a real lift to the family.

We also got informed that as from today any mail going off was to be censored! This meant that anything that we wrote, could and would be read before being sent off to our nearest and dearest. The Padre and a couple of others were detailed off to go through our letters before they were sent off to the UK. This was because some pillock had heard about the D-Day date and had thought he was important by letting those at home know! It still amazes me to this day, that somebody can be as daft as that without realising they were putting 28,000 lives at risk! I know I may have had a head start being a communicator (you had to have a degree of intelligence to do this job), but it is common sense. Wherever you go in basic training, there are posters all over the place "Careless talk costs lives." This was the days of the IRA and I know the Bootnecks weren't as hated as the Paras by the IRA, but they should have known better, one of them must have let the date out of the bag from overhearing a conversation in the Amphibious Operations Room, and the 'buzz' on the ship was that it was a Royal that had done it!

Tues 20th
Canberra & Elk joined us at around 07:00z of Ascension. Stacks of v.s. Still very quiet.

We turned the Elk, a Roll OnRoll Off (RO-RO) ferry, into a flight deck. Our Chief Stoker and some of his team went over and cut the sides of the ship, opening up the upper scupper to become a flight deck! Not sure of the shipping company that owned the ship or that they would be happy to know we were doing this to her, but I watched fascinated as they cut away at the metal and let it drop over the side. It was an innovative piece of engineering and design – amazing what Matelots can do when the need arises! No potential employer should ever turn one down for a job, because they can turn their hands to most things and are very flexible in their approach and attitude to work!

Wed 21st
Still not a lot happening. Had a RAS (L) (fuel) at about 22:30.
Did a 'Vertrep'. Was stores party.

See what I mean about 'Day Worker'? I had to be on watch for the RAS, even though I should have finished at 17:00. It really didn't take long for that idea to fall by the wayside!

I was also to discover much later in communication with the Navigator Commander John Prime, that the RAS took much longer than normal, as Fearless was down to 29% fuel and we also lost a boiler on approach to the RAS. It took so long, that we had to do a one hundred and eighty degree turn to get us back on track. So my day working became a very long day indeed!

Thurs 22nd
All quiet on the home front!

Fri 23rd
Saw loads of Dolphins in the sea playing about. And also 1 Hammer head. Got recognition training. No I

haven't! It's just been cancelled!

Sat 24th

Nothing happening. Band concert from 'Booties' of Canberra. (Boring!).

If nothing else, the Band Concert was an excuse for a few beers. The Royals put their heart and soul into the concert, turning out in full rig and doing a real 'Last Night at The Proms' affair. I think I was a bit young to really appreciate it; or I may have been put off for life by my Dad, who used to play military band music on the Radiogram at full volume when he came home from the Sergeant's Mess on a Saturday and Sunday afternoon whilst we were in Germany. Probably the former, as I now own a Massed Bands of The Royal Marines Beating The Retreat CD!

Captain Jeremy Larken writing in 'Tales from the Hot Seat', 'During a trip to the Caribean earlier in the year... We embarked for a short visit the Commander-in-Chief, Admiral Sir John Fieldhouse. He enjoyed a traditional ship's company concert held on the vehicle (ro-ro) decks, in which five hundred voices nearly lifted the flight deck heavenwards with 'Hearts of Oak' and 'Rule Britannia'.

The Admiral turned to me and said, without conceivable premonition, "What if we were to go to war tomorrow?" and then, referring to the same concert mentioned in my diary 'We took the morale pulse from day to day. One evening during our three week pause at Ascension Island, the very same Royal Marine band that had unleashed such carefree enthusiasm but two months previously boarded to give a concert. The event was well-attended but subdued. Concerned at first, I concluded correctly that sober stock was being taken of our prospects. We accepted that our likely fate was to sail south to the Falklands, to face hazards new to us all.'

So perhaps the concert wasn't boring at all. Just that our thoughts were probably somewhere else.

6

Sloppiness

Sun 25th

Argy merchant ship sighted (first reported by me!). No notice taken of it. It hung around about 7 miles from us. Sent a Lynx off Antelope to investigate. Then sent Antelope to shadow. It soon disappeared. Also great news! South Georgia regained by SAS, SBS & Booties. Argy Sub Santa Fe, damaged in air attack - now in our hands. Looks like it will be over before we get there!

This incident really pissed me off big time! I was an excellent look-out, and would often spot ships over the horizon before our radar operators got them on their screens. This was one such incident, and much has been made of it in the many books that have been written about the Falklands War. Here is Commodore Michael Clapps' (on board HMS Fearless at the time) version of events from AMPHIBIOUS ASSAULT FALKLAND ISLANDS – The Battle of San Carlos Water:

'...On this day, the Argentine Government-owned merchant ship, Rio de la Plata, was spotted off the north-west coast by the British Administrator from his house. It turned out that she had been seen earlier off the north-west by Canberra. I dispatched a Sea King to investigate followed by Antelope who escorted the merchant ship to the south-west. Although unlikely, it was quite possible that she had launched some saboteurs but, more importantly, she would have assessed the size and structure of our Amphibious Group and if she had been listening to radio transmissions would have been able to collect some important intelligence.'

Let me put the record straight! I was now back on the watch keeping rota and was doing the Long Morning 02:00 – 08:00. Off Ascension Island this wasn't that bad as it was warm and balmy through the early hours of the morning. The night was just moving into dawn, the dark ink blue sky was just starting to change into the clear blue of the day. The sun wasn't yet coming over the horizon, but the daylight was starting to break. Visibility was excellent and the azure blue of the sea and ink blue sky were starting to merge. I was wandering around the signal decks and bridge wings, when at about 04:00 I saw something dark out on the horizon. It broke up the merging sky and sea, as a slim dark streak between them. I looked through my binoculars to see if I could get a clearer view. It was black smoke! I moved over to one of the internal intercom units, never taking my eyes of the horizon;

>"Bridge this Port signal deck. Black smoke on the horizon bearing red 110"
>
>"Roger signal deck. Keep an eye on it!" came the response.

I continued my wanderings and about 30 minutes later, reported the superstructure; it was a bit hazy and just visible as it was coming over the horizon. I called it in again this time asking to exchange IDs. Not yet came the response. I'm assuming the OOW had checked with the 'Plot' in the Ops room to see if they had picked anything up. I don't think they had. 20 minutes later, I reported in that it looked like some type of Fleet Auxiliary Vessel and I didn't recognise it. I knew we were not expecting any to join us that day. Still no real response from the bridge. I was now starting to get a bit worried. We had recently had a bollocking for not taking this situation seriously, and here I was watching some sort of foreign Auxiliary vessel appear over the horizon, heading in the general direction of 30 or more ships at a vital anchorage and preparing for war! A few rounds here, a few missiles there, a tiny submersible with a couple of divers could have destroyed our whole fleet, and nothing was being done about it! I didn't have the authority to just jump on the light and exchange IDs so I was waiting for the order to do so.

Suddenly all hell broke loose. The Captain and Commodore rushed to the bridge with their various entourages and lots of questions as to why this ship hadn't been challenged and allowed to get this close. It appears (from what I have read), that the local Governor of Ascension had woken up and seen this ship from his window. He had a hot line to Sandy Woodward on the Hermes, who immediately dispatched a Lynx to investigate the ship and HMS Antelope the Type 21 Frigate to chase it away. It got within 7 miles! I saw it over 22 miles away (over the horizon) and had been constantly reporting it and my concerns, which were ignored.

The helicopter reported that there were a couple of canoes arranged on the flight deck. These could have been used by Special Forces, and no doubt they were on board that ship, to get close enough to our fleet to get in the water and plant limpets on the hulls of the ships at anchor.

The Argy Skipper and crew must have thought all their birthdays had come at once. Getting so close would also have given them an opportunity to report on what ships, the size of the force and how lax we were in our approach to war.

Once the chopper had got overhead and it saw a Type 21 at full steam heading towards it, it turned tail and sailed back home to report what it had just discovered.

I was bloody furious that all my reports had been ignored, and we had been put at such risk due to the laziness and incompetence of the OOW.

Within 30 minutes of it being chased off, divers were in the water checking the hulls of the ships (what a job in such beautiful, clear seas, notwithstanding the sharks) to make sure nothing had been attached. All ships had at least one ship's diver on board and every ship was checked. On completion of that, we started dropping flash charges into the sea to deter any divers that may have got off the Argentine ship. These were very loud bangers dropped over the side, and could be heard reverberating around the ship every time one went off. The basic idea was to blow the ear drums of any divers as the sound and shock waves are magnified under water.

Fortunately, nothing came of this except that we had to set off for sea every night and return to anchor at first light in the morning. It was tiring, unproductive and interruptive to the ship's company, making extra work, because someone was too lazy to listen to a young 18-year-old signalman. I was good at ship recognition as well as look-out and knew from the start this ship was not one of ours.

Read what you like into the 'dit' above, but that is what happened and that ship was spotted, reported several times and tracked by me for hours before a third party had to intervene. I don't know if any other lookouts on the other ships had the same problems as me in getting believed or if indeed they had even seen it and reported it.

The good news of the day was that South Georgia had been recovered. South Georgia was the first island about 300 miles south-east of the Falkland Islands and a British Dependency. It was recovered by the Special Air Service and Royal Marines with the support of HMS Antrim's Wessex Helicopters, and HMS Yarmouth in support of her with NGS.

In those days, the SAS always knew best and had to find the hardest way to get onto the island. This entailed landing on a glacier against all the advice given by the 'Senior Service' and making their way down it to get to the Argentine Base. We lost 2 Wessex helicopters in this folly, fortunately no deaths. It turned out alright in the end, but what a waste of time and key pieces of equipment!

I noted that 'it would all be over before we get there.' I didn't really believe it, but there was no harm in hoping.

Mon 26th

Sonar contact! At 00:15z, called to Action Stations (first real ones). Was crashed out! We immediately set off to sea for night. Had Action Stations for 2 1/4 hours, then had morning. At first thought was sub, but nothing happened.

There were to be a lot of Sonar and Air contacts called during the whole period. Many turned out to be spurious, or whales; other sonar contacts were identified as probably Soviet Submarines. The Russians were having a field day with all this British activity going on as they hadn't seen such a force since the Second World War! It was an ideal opportunity for them to collect intelligence about the ships, their engine and prop sounds (their signature). We also had Russian intelligence vessels hanging around.

The air contacts were called and often were just large seagulls, but again we had Russian Bears – Long-Range Bombers – over-flying and circling us quite brazenly. There was nothing we could do about this, but we hoped they were not passing vital information to the Argentines.

7

Death at Sea

Wed 4th May
General Belgrano sunk. 400 blokes killed?

I didn't know what else to write in my diary. It was such a shock.

The Captain somberly made the announcement that the Belgrano had been sunk by torpedoes fired from HMS Conqueror and we were unaware of what had happened to any survivors. He emphasised the fact that many sailors could possibly have died and many more were at risk of freezing to death, and discouraged the crew from any jingoistic celebration around the sinking. We were all at a heightend state emotionally and no matter what the Captain said, you could hear the cheers around the ship at the news! I joined in at first; it was exciting news and not something we were expecting. Some of the mess and crew were convinced that the Argentineans would give up and go home. It would all be over before we got down there and we would just strengthen the barracks to protect the Islands.

I quickly felt very unnerved about the sinking, not

because it was wrong, as far as I was concerned we were at war and the Belgrano and Vinciento de May were our biggest threats at sea next to the Super Entendard and Exocet; but because there were hundreds of men floating around somewhere in the South Atlantic, freezing to death, drowning or burning from the explosions. They were sailors like us and no one wants to die this way. Two of my biggest fears have always been death by drowning or being burnt to death. I tried not to imagine how those poor blokes were feeling out there in the cruel sea, but I was unable to completely block out my feelings about it. Others were obviously thinking this as well because the ship became very quiet for the next few hours. This could be us as we make our way down or if we get attacked. What will happen to us should it happen? I think this is why I only wrote 6 words. It was a shock, very frightening and very real. This bought the reality home of what we were doing and it scared me. The Captain continued to keep us updated almost hourly with what was happening with the rescue operation.

Through the night we were receiving signal traffic about the incident from the Conqueror, and what really shocked and angered us the most, was the fact that the Belgrano's escorts had run and abandoned those poor lads to die in freezing seas. I understand there is an unwritten rule (it may be part of the Geneva Convention) within the Submarine service that once a ship has been hit and is sinking, they do not then interfere with the rescue effort and would never fire on any unit participating in a rescue. The escorts didn't even search for the submarine. In fact, they didn't return until days later, although fortunately some survivors were found and rescued. We knew then what sort of people we were dealing with - selfish cowards who didn't give a damn about their own.

This was a real eye opener and nobody could understand why anybody would treat their shipmates like this. I know the submarine threat was still there, but a decent Captain would take the risk with his ship to help those in peril; taking the chance that the Captain of the submarine was also a gentleman who would not fire again whilst a rescue operation was taking place.

Wed 5th

HMS Sheffield lost. Sunk by an Argy Exocet. Ops rm/ MCO complex (part of my area) hit 30 (strike that) 20 killed. Since 26th we have been going to sea every night and sometimes anchoring during the day. Started going 1 in 2 defence (type) watches. Bought a watch - £62.00 Seiko. Also 1 Harrier gone.

I was horrified when I heard this news. The whole ship was in a state of total shock. This really turned our views on them giving up upside down. I knew now that this was for real and we were going to have to fight to the death to win the Falklands back. It also created a sense of "We'll get these bastards back. They cannot get away with this." Everybody was baying for blood. Our shipmates had been killed or injured now, and we had a steely resolve for revenge. Hatred appeared to suddenly grow amongst us.

All I could think of was those poor blokes being caught in the blast and the flames; the way they died so horribly. Those that were still alive had to fight their way out of the ship through the thick, cloying smoke with their injuries, and their burnt flesh. It was an awful picture in my mind's eye and, once again, played on my biggest fears of being burnt alive or drowning as I listened to announcements over the tannoy about shipmates in our Task Force being injured and dying in just these circumstances.

As I said in the introduction, this diary was written as it happened. Today's entry was a classic example. The initial reports received about losses were 30 killed. As I was writing this, an announcement was made updating us on the situation and thankfully the number was far less than first feared.

I have always loved being out in the open, which was one of the reasons why I chose to become a Tactical Radio Operator, so I could be on the bridge and outside on the wings and signal decks. During our communication training at Mercury, if you scored over 95% in your Morse exams in part 2 training, you were automatically selected for Submarine service. Three of us in my class got 95% plus and I was proud to have achieved 97%. I had to fight to stay out of submarines. The thought of being encased underwater for months at a time filled me with dread and I was sent to the Kelly Squadron office to argue my case. I eventually won, but only after threatening to leave the RN. The thought of being under water really did terrify me that much.

The area of the Sheffield that took a severe amount of damage was the area of the ship that I worked in as part of the watch system. We would alternate between the bridge, Ops room and Main Communication Office (MCO) through our watches. I decided there and then that when the balloon went up I would be on the upper scupper and avoid being below decks at all costs. I really did not want to die in the bowels of the ship. If we were hit and the need arose, I could leap over the side without struggling through the dark passage ways and ladders etc. I could also see what was happening if I was up top! I needed to be out in the open and not cooped up inside a steel vessel, submarine or ship, I had to be on the upper scupper and the 'Shiny Sheff' incident made that all the clearer to me.

As for the £62.00 Seiko, it was that or a Mickey Mouse watch. We have to record times that we receive signals by light or transmit them. I never had a watch, and always relied on my oppo to record the time. Due to how busy we were I didn't always have an oppo with me, so I had to buy a watch. The NAAFI had two left Mickey or Seiko. It was a lot of money to spend in those days; I only got paid about £35.00 a week. I still have the receipt and I still have the watch. I wear it through April to June and on any parades that I go on. I've had two watches my whole adult life, that one and one my children bought me for my 40th Birthday – a Seiko very similar to the original, which I wear on a day to day basis.

8

Fearless and Me

Thur 6th May

Did a Vertrep in afternoon. Wrote another 'maily' for home (have to remember to get stamps). **Atlantic Conveyor** *joined with its Harriers. Also* **Intrepid** *has joined.* **Atlantic Conveyor** *first sighted during middle by me and reported. Nothing happened, about 5 o'clock, it was about 2 miles away from us and the OOW decided (at last!) to exchange IDs. 2nd OOW came out looking for the Seaman look-out and started to tick him off for not reporting it, but I interrupted & told him it was reported during middle. His face dropped & he had to apologise. Diary's getting a bit tatty, will have to take more care of it.*

N.B. It's the first time Intrepid & Fearless have been together in the amphibious role since Aden.

Another frustrating encounter with OOW and yet again, my reports were ignored as I watched the Atlantic Conveyor sailing in. We had to wait to be ordered to challenge anything or send signals. This was one of the biggest STUFT (Ships Taken Up From Trade) to be part of the fleet and she was carrying vital supplies of Chinook Helicopters and Harriers, plus tons of other kit and equipment that were needed for our war efforts at sea and ashore. The STUFT had an RN crew on board as well as civilian so they knew the routine and every ship had an RN Comms team with them. I did the necessary for the identification, and reported it in. The 2nd OOW then came out on the wings to have a go at the Seaman Gunners. I was furious, and stepped in: "Sir, check the RO's log, you'll find it was reported by me several hours ago, and ignored by the OOW. Don't take it out on us!"

The middle is 00:01 (there is no 00:00 in the Royal Navy) to 04:00, though in this instance we were on 'long watches' which meant they were 6 hours long not four. His face really was a picture, but he did have the decency to say sorry.

The Fearless has been linked with my life in quite a spooky way, which may explain why I have such strong feelings about her (apart from the great ship's company).

She was launched 6th December 1963 – I was born 1st December 1963. In November 1967, with HMS Intrepid, she was in Aden withdrawing the troops from the uprising and the independence of Aden (South Yemen). Guess where I was. At 3 years old, living in married quarters in Aden at war being shot at!

In those days, families went into war zones. We lived in Aden for a couple of years where, Mum tells me, rebels regularly carried out drive-by shootings at the married quarters. She also tells a story of when I was back in the UK shortly after we got back from Aden, and I was out with Grandad ('Quare Fella', was his nickname for me, I was his little shadow and worshipped him); he went to kick a tin we found lying on the ground and I grabbed his hand and pulled him back, telling him "You mustn't do that because you can die."

This shocked and saddened him that someone so young, who should be innocent and able to have fun in the streets, should think like that. The rebels would throw grenades or set booby traps, such as tins left lying around, with explosives and nails in them that would detonate if disturbed (now known as IEDs). We Army kids were taught what we should look out for and what we shouldn't touch, which also carried on in Germany and with the troubles in Northern Ireland.

I think it was at this point that I also wrote the classic letter to a loved one, "This may be my last opportunity to tell you I love you…"

I had been madly in love with a girl called Paula since I returned back to Millom School in 1977. During school she was going out with someone else but she was brilliant, and we laughed and had fun in classes. I eventually got to go out with her after we left school and I was based in Chatham, so it was a long-distance relationship that lasted 3 beautiful months. She ended the relationship one weekend, citing too much pressure. She never elaborated on the pressure and we were both in tears when she told me. I was devastated.

This night I had to write to her to tell her how I felt. I genuinely meant everything I said in the letter and poured my heart out to her. I told her that I may never see her again or ever get the chance to tell her how I had felt about her for so long. It took me ages to write the letter. I really was struggling with my emotions because I felt so strongly about her and I was sailing into a war not knowing what was going to happen or if I was going to survive. Paula wrote back to me telling me that the letter had her in tears and she wanted to keep in touch. This really lifted my spirits and my morale. She gave me some hope that perhaps when this was all over, if I survived, there was a chance we would get back together again. We exchanged several letters during the war, and we did try to get together later. She really did help me get through it, and, I hope she knows how much I appreciate what she did for me during that very difficult time. She was not able to join my homecoming party, as she had booked a holiday away in Torquay with friends. If I had come home a day earlier she would have been there. We tried later through the months after I came home to see each other, but I had started drinking heavily and my behaviour was somewhat erratic during those months; we always ended up arguing and things were never right again.

9

On Our Way

Fri 7th

After 21 days of waiting at Ascension, we finally set sail at 20:00z. All very quiet.

It really was very quiet! With all that had happened in the past 3 days with the Belgrano and Sheffield, I think we were all in a state of shock. I was certainly feeling very unnerved about what was going to happen next. Although we were sailing as a Task Group, we were an amphibious force with very little air support or other quick response ships to protect us. We were the centre of the formation, with the LSLs covering the outside as we were a principal ship and needed protection. It was quiet and we sailed away silently with our amphibious ships towards the Falklands at last.

Sat 8th

Had Action Stations at 08:20z secured at 10:30z, but stayed up top on watch. Had Dogs, did 4 hrs in Ops rm, really boring as we are totally silent - even radar to shake of Russian AGI. 12 mile exclusion zone enforced. Watched Return of the Pink Panther.

We sailed under total silence. To assist the silent transit, there had already been a navigation plan laid out and this was signalled to all ships to be executed without further orders. This meant that the ships' Captains carried out major manoeuvres without being told again.

It was amazing. Many manoeuvres of the group were carried out by flashing light or flag signal. We would send the signal down the line and it was relayed 'Flag L' by all ships. The signal would be hoisted on the yardarm, repeated by the next ship and followed all the way along. Then executed and the ships would turn together. It was truly amazing to carry out everything we were trained to do and see it in action.

The downside to silent transit was that the Tactical Operators also had to take turns in the Ops room, where we would monitor the circuits and, if necessary, take over if the bridge was wiped out. This was a great job whilst it was busy, but boring as hell in silent routine for obvious reasons – nothing was happening. I hated this. I disliked being inside the ship at the best of times, but doing nothing didn't help my attitude. At times, we were not even allowed to read books to keep us occupied, just sit there and listen to nothing.

The Russian AGI had been hanging around for ages. There was nothing we could do about it, but try to leave it behind. We were still in the era of the Cold War, and this was the greatest opportunity any enemy could have to see how a NATO force operated in a genuine war footing. We had Bear Deltas, massive silver aircraft, couldn't have been more than a thousand feet above us! Casually circling over our heads in slow, lazy turns. Long-range reconnaissance aircraft blatantly over-flying us, looking incredibly impressive; submarines underneath us; and the AGIs, which looked like trawlers, with a lot of aerials and radar displays on their upper scupper, watching our every move. We suspected that they were passing information to the Argentines, and took every step we could to reduce any info they could pick up; although I'm not sure if it was ever proven that they had passed info, or were just gathering for their own needs.

Before we sailed, we asked Wideawake, to record twenty-four hours of Ship to Shore 'chatter' (Radio Traffic), and to play it back before we sailed. This was an attempt to give us breathing space from the AGI as we slipped silently away, whilst all normal traffic was bouncing around the airwaves. It seemed to work.

10

Am I Already Dead?

Tues 11th

*3 days space of quiet. But today everything started to happen. Got turned in for 24 hrs (Mon night) with sinusitis (or something like that), then at 01:30z had exercise Action Stns. All closed up & ready in 12 1/2 minutes (very commendable), but CY (Ten Bellies) Mouter told me I had to do my watch (long morning). Still in agony, but TB took no notice, not even with sick note, so did watch. Had afternoon during which time 2 Russian Bear Deltas reconnaissance aircraft flew over our Task Group & circled. Obviously taking stacks of phots and passing info to Argies. Then at about 14:30z, Action Stations for real as a periscope was sighted by Intrepid and so the Task Group split with **Ardent** & **Argonaut** going to investigate sighting, & 5 Sea Kings. Turned out to be a school of whales (we think), but did have positive sonar contacts. Capt. reckons probably a Russian so no threat to us. Argy fuel tanker blown up by Arrow in Falkland Sound.*

Had an airdrop from a Hercules containing mail. Got 1 maily of Kim but nothing else.

(perhaps they already think that I'm already dead so aren't bothering anymore.)

Night time all quiet.

N.B. Took just 8 mins to get closed up for Action Stns (superb)!

Also, had a fire on board and when alarm sounded, we were all up & ready to go to A/S (as General alarm and fire alarm same), but only small lagging fire and put out quickly by fire party. Were ready in 3 minutes!

Sinusitis read as migraine. The scab lifters couldn't put a name to what I was suffering with. A stabbing pain in my temples, blind in one eye, slurred speech and numb right hand. I was in agony and unable to operate effectively. It was only an exercise but the Yeoman wanted me on the bridge. I believed he was a vindictive bastard, but he was just driving us to experience extremes, because if the crap really hit the fan, migraine or no migraine, I would have to operate at some level. As hard as it was I got through it.

The Bear Delta's a massive silver aircraft, couldn't have been more than a thousand feet above us! Casually circling over our heads in slow, lazy turns. They were an impressive sight, and there was nothing we could do about them, but watch and wave as they did their bidding. We were still in international waters and they knew exactly what they were doing. A fantastic opportunity for all of us to get a good look at each other!

We got a lot of spurious contacts, from sonar, radar and visual. People were jittery and no one was taking any chances. Even if it was the Intrepid calling contact, we had to take it seriously. Away went the anti-submarine ships, but they ended up chasing a pod of whales. A positive sonar had been achieved, though wasn't consistent; it was possibly another Russian checking us out.

We were already at Defence Watches, so half the ship's company were on watch, the other half getting their heads down or relaxing. When the claxon sounded for Action Stations, everybody moved! We had been practicing this ever since we sailed from Portsmouth and I think the effect of the Belgrano and Sheffield incidents really affected us all. We knew this was for real and everybody took it seriously. We were up and ready to fight in under 8 minutes – not bad for six-hundred-plus crew! We were really impressed with ourselves and I felt that I was part of a great team that could do anything.

In all this time away, I got very few letters from home. It was really starting to hurt. Kim was the only constant in my life at this point, as she regularly responded to my letters. I had sent many home, in fact I wrote home nearly every day to keep the family updated on what was happening. I'd describe the scenery, the things the lads did in the mess, on watch, what we had for scran, how many cups of tea or coffee I made throughout the day, just to keep in contact. Some of it must have been really dull, but to me it was the most important stuff in the world, because I was talking to my family who I may never see again. But they weren't talking back!

I was trying to stay strong and not let it get to me. I used to lie in my pit at night and listen to some of the other lads quietly snuffling, sometimes sobbing, as they read letters from loved ones, or listened to tapes on their Sony Walkmans that they had received from girlfriends, or their children. One night after the long first, I listened to one lad for nearly fifteen minutes. It was heart breaking. I really felt for them, and wanted to say something to support them; it was, and always has been, in my nature to care. I couldn't though because these were very private moments. They thought people around them were asleep and they had the time to themselves to let some of their emotions free. My emotions were all over the place. How could they forget their 'little Kevin Tops' (my childhood nickname as I used to have very blond curly hair as a young child), the child they had so emotionally waved off to war only a few weeks before? I wanted to scream and cry to let all my frustrations out. My thoughts were disjointed and irrational. They had never really loved me after all. They didn't care about me. I was nothing to them really. I was out of sight out of mind. I hurt so much every time I didn't get a letter from home.

On this day I didn't even believe I had a family. I really did feel that they had already written me off for dead. It was an awful feeling to have, and it tore my heart and soul right to the core.

A few days later, I hastily scribbled the comment out in the diary in thick black biro, as sacks of delayed 'mailies' arrived on board, and weeks of heartache and pain suddenly evaporated.

My Dad wrote two letters separately, I put all the letters in post-date order to read them. The first was written a couple of days after I had left home. He wrote "Please forgive me, for being such a silly old fool. It was just the frustration and tears of being an old soldier who is too old and no longer wanted or needed to fight!" referring to my departure. Mum told me later, "that he couldn't bear the thought of his son going to war without him. He felt I was just a boy, and not designed or mentally ready to fight a war; it should be him out there, not you."

His second letter included a telling off for writing a letter home addressed to Mrs J. Porter, "There are no secrets between us and the correct title in the address is Mr & Mrs P.J.A. Porter!" That was me told! I always used the correct form of address after that and wrote back to both of them in the same letter. I don't think I ever told them how I was feeling and certainly never how bad I felt this day in my writings home. It was many, many years before I talked about it to them.

FEARLESS - The Diary of an 18 Year Old at War in the Falklands

11

Air Drops

Wed 12th

Did a RAS (L) with Tidepool (courtesy of the Chileans!). Another airdrop at approx. 13:00z. 1,200 miles from Falklands and @ 15 knots approx.should be there between 6 - 8 days all being well. (Air drop just been delayed till 11:30 tomorrow). General alarm & fire alarm have now been given a separate sound. (Change of pen). 2 Argy bombers shot down by Glasgow which sustained little damage (a couple of 3ft holes above water line). Wrote a maily home. 1 SK lost, but crew safe.

Like many of the Royal Naval fleet and support ships, the Tidepool (fuel tanker) was about to be scrapped under a very cutting defence review in which the Navy was about to take the brunt. John Nott had a lot to answer for! Fearless was earmarked for the scrap heap, and it was only after some very impressive demonstrations of her might and the power of persuasion of Commodore Michael Clapp, Major General Julian Thompson and Captain Larken during an exercise off Browndown Camp in the Solent the previous year, that she was saved. The picture Rear Admiral Larken has provided for the foreword really demonstrates her versatility, and of course we had a brilliant crew worked up in very short order! The RFA Tidepool had not been so lucky and had been sold to the Chileans for some ridiculously low price.

The Chileans were not the best of mates with Argentina. They were constantly at loggerheads over who owned the Beagle Straits, a stretch of water that ran between them and gave access from the Atlantic to the Pacific. Strangely enough Argentina claimed they owned it. Anyway back to the sale, Chile agreed to delay the delivery of the Tidepool, so we could use her down South. This was a real boost to our war effort and ensured that we had enough fuel for the Task Force to get to the Islands (not all in Tidepool, but she did her bit).

Airdrops were a source of major anticipation for everyone. Mail would usually be included in these. For others, it was the joy of getting into the sea boat to go and retrieve the cartons that were dropped into the sea. Putting one of those into a South Atlantic swell took some skill. Spotting the canisters, steering and controlling the small open craft, took even more. An RO always had to go with them to man the portable radio. It was quite hair-raising and at times very dangerous but at 18, always a laugh!

The Glasgow was attacked during a Naval Gunfire Barrage on Argentine positions. She took out a couple of planes, and the report we got was that she had minor damage. I cannot even remember if there were any casualties announced during this attack and again it was a very throw away entry in my diary; a marked example of my immaturity at the time, though never intended to diminish the seriousness of those incidents.

The helicopter fleet were working overtime. It seemed

they were constantly in the air passing between ships, delivering stores, personnel, ferrying senior officers to various briefings. They were real work horses, but sadly with so much time in the air, things were bound to happen. The loss of any unit during war is bad enough, but to lose them as you are preparing for war meant that the Command had to make alternative plans and sadly sometimes lives were lost. This time we were fortunate.

Thur 13th
Another air drop, but was delayed (yet again!). Didn't happen till 13:00. No mail. Anti-flash, flak jackets and tin helmets to be worn all the time whilst on the signal deck. Only 900 miles from the Falklands & within bombing range of Argy bombers. Nearly lost a Sea King with engine failure. It was full of people (13) and was bought back on deck with one engine with no casualties. The Padre was in it - maybe that was the reason!

The helicopters were really taking a pounding out in the South Atlantic. The flying hours that were being put in before the campaign started were nothing compared to what they were going to do when we got to the Islands. Tasks had to be carried out, and the air crews were worked tirelessly to ensure the aircraft were fit to fly. They could not anticipate every eventuality that these helicopters would encounter and, on this day, it became a standing joke that the 'God Botherer' was on board which saved the aircraft! Even so, it was a very nervous period, looking out for the craft and guiding it back on board safely, and the relief was palpable, when it landed safely with no casualties.

We were now considered to be in range of Argentine air attacks and, after the disaster of the Sheffield, the

Command was taking no chances. I think putting us into action gear from this stage on was also a tactic to keep the crews aware of what we were about to encounter. Wearing the kit certainly made me feel that things were getting serious, and my senses were heightened with the tension of knowing that any moment we could come under attack.

Fri 14th
A quiet day today. Weather definitely changing and it's getting colder. Had another airdrop but no mail, only flak jackets. Don't expect mail for a while yet. Now 1200 miles away – Captain's made a boo-boo!

Not sure what happened with the navigation on this day, but there was a definite pipe on the 13th that we were only nine hundred miles away! I recall that the Captain said that he had given incorrect information the day before. The Navigator was pretty good at what he did, and he informs me that it could have been a change of plan into the holding area or just a 'slip of the tongue'. Definatley not a navigation error! I'm glad they got it all sorted before we got too close, or we would have sailed straight past the islands!

12

SBS, SAS & Pebble Island

Sat 15th

Fairly quiet. Yet another emergency landing, but no one hurt again & the helo landed on Atlantic Conveyor's deck & not ours, but it was our helo. Argy Boeing 707 surveillance aircraft detected 68 miles from the TG, but it didn't get any nearer, obviously didn't detect us, & slowly got further away. Had a RAS(S) with **Stromness**, *had to break away & start again. Weather definitely deteriorating, starting to get slightly rougher with 'goffas' coming over the bows. Wrote another maily to Kim. Mail closes at 0130z in morning (tomorrow)! Pebble Island attacked & sabotaged by SBS. Planes (11) and ammo dump destroyed. SBS had been on Island for 10 days.*

It was handy having so many landing pads so far out at sea. The elements really do take their toll on the aircraft and, at times, they were overloaded so incidents were bound to happen. We really needed our helicopters for the landings and supplies and transportation when the troops were ashore. Fortunately, most ended favourably on someone else's deck and rarely in the sea.

The Argentine Boeing 707 had been detected on a number of occasions. It was always just out of Sea Dart range, though Harriers had been scrambled to intercept it. We didn't attack it because we couldn't be sure that it wasn't a civilian aircraft, or certain that no civvies were on board. Its signature was that of a passenger jet and not a military. The fallout if we had attacked a civilian aircraft in international (though it was now a maritime exclusion zone) waters would not have helped our cause at the United Nations or with the rest of the world. Whether it had detected the Task Force I'll never know; I think when I wrote '...obviously didn't detect us', it was at the least wishful thinking on my part and more than probably re-enforcing the story that the Argentines weren't really a professional force, and therefore incompetent. This made me feel better and safer.

Having crossed the Equator and now firmly in the South Atlantic, the seas started to get rougher. I can't really remember all the heavy seas that have been reported and seen in some of the dramatic news footage of the Task Force at sea. I don't believe we hit that many on transit. Most of the footage seen was probably filmed during our time in San Carlos, whilst the main Task Force remained fifty plus miles further out and therefore got hammered by the strong winds, whilst we got hammered by the Argentine Air Force.

The rough seas obviously brought problems for ships when carrying out a RAS. Bringing two ships within fifty ft of each other, travelling at 10 knots and being connected by a couple of ropes and fuel pipes is difficult enough without rolling around in crashing waves. During workups in Portland, RASs are always practised and emergency breakaways are part of this. The weather was such that it was causing problems and the pipes were in danger of breaking apart, as well as the ships coming a little too close during the manoeuvre. When a decision to break away is made, it all happens very quickly, with very few people in the connecting areas. If it is the weather or swell that is causing the problems, another course is set that the ships have to steer on, and then we reform and start again. It is a major skill of seamanship and control by the Command of both ships and a very impressive sight to see. In the early eighties, there were very few navies that could carry out this manoeuvre and the Russians had not been able to perfect it at this stage, so this gave us a bit of a tactical advantage, in that we did not have to stop for hours in the middle of the sea to refuel.

The Argentinians had trained at Portland in 1981. The Santisma Trinidad, a Type 42 Destroyer the same as HMS Sheffield, was 'worked up' by the FOST (Flag Officer Sea Training) team. I do not know if we give non-NATO forces the same training as our own fleet but, if we did, the Argentinians had probably practised RAS whilst they were being trained by us. We had sold one of our Royal Fleet Auxiliary tankers to the Chilean Navy, so I assume that the South Americans were able to RAS. This would have given their ships longer at sea if they had been brave enough to come out and face us, rather than run and hide after the Belgrano sinking. It was a relief that their Navy stayed alongside, leaving the fight to the Air Force and Army during the war, because any distraction amongst the Task Force at sea would probably have affected the air cover we needed over the Falklands.

The Pebble Island raid was probably one of the biggest shocks to the Argentines next to the bombing by the Vulcans. It told them, in no uncertain terms, "THE BRITISH HAVE LANDED!"

A team of SBS (SBS in my diary though it was actually a mix of SBS/SAS) was secreted ashore and made their way to a very important landing strip which had eleven Pucara Ground Attack aircraft based on it, plus a base for a number of Argentine soldiers and airmen. The SBS planted explosives on every plane and destroyed each one almost simultaneously. Not one of the SBS men was injured or killed, all returning to the ship safely. The attack saved a lot of lives because it put the airstrip out of action and reduced the Argentine short range air attack capability.

The results of this audacious attack were announced over the tannoy to huge cheers around the ship.

The SBS (Special Boat Squadron) are the Royal Navy's equivalent of the SAS (Special Air Service) and were relatively unknown, unlike the SAS who had their moment of worldwide glory when they carried out the dramatic rescue of the Iranian Embassy Hostages in London in 1980. The Embassy rescue was filmed live, and the world witnessed the men clad in black, with black balaclavas, as they abseiled down the side of the building, crashed through the windows, hurled flash bangs and smoke into the Embassy, killing all but one of the terrorists with no injuries to any of the hostages or themselves. That day the SAS proved what a powerful force Britain could be.

The SBS are equally as impressive and active as the SAS, but had not been as widely publicised until this day. It was probably one of the most daring raids carried out by the Special Forces since the Second World War, and it had a devastating effect on the Argentines, and an even better effect on our morale!

13

The Torture Factor

Sun 16th
LSLs, Antrim (DLG) *joined & a few Merchant ships,*
now have nineteen ships in our TG at the moment.

Whilst we were sailing south, I kept a record of the
names, times and dates of all ships joining the Task Force.
As we got closer our security briefs increased; these
revealed the Argentine military's torture techniques,
how they treated their civilian population, and their own
armed forces. We had to remove all our branch badges
from our uniforms and were briefed that should we be
captured as RO's, we were to maintain that we were
Seamen Operators. , I also decided to tear the pages out
that had the details of the ships written on them. I had it
in my mind that, if captured, I would have my diary on me
and the information it contained would have given the
Argentines a huge amount of intelligence regarding our
Task Force. It would almost certainly have given away my
position within the ship; even though I was only a junior
rating, I had access to secret information and, in my mind,
the Argentinian Junta would see me as a prime target for
torture. We were hearing stories of the disappearance of
young men who disagreed with them so I was naturally

fearful of what would they do to me, an enemy and a communicator, someone who 'may' have knowledge of what was happening and what future plans we may have. It didn't cross my mind that if we had been sunk, and had to abandon ship, that the diary would have been destroyed in the water! Admittedly I did carry it in a sealed plastic bag in my respirator bag, carried it everywhere with me 24 hours a day, and wrote in it whenever I got an opportunity. Somehow I foolishly believed the plastic bag would protect it! However, I desperately wanted to hand it to my Dad and I believe that is what I had in my mind all the time that I was down there – I had to save the diary no matter what! So it made sense to tear out the intel in the back.

Mon 17th

Exercise Action Stns at 09:00, had ex fire on bridge. Poss sub detected by Argonaut, but only rocks on the bottom of sea. Argy Boeing 707 detected yet again but nothing happened. Also C130 Hercules detected, thought was Argy but turned out to be one of ours. Apart from that all quiet so far (20:48). Weather's getting worse and it's absolutely freezing up top. Anti-Flash to be worn relaxed (hoods round neck & gloves to hand) at all times between decks in case of missile attack, because fire ball of explosions will burn face badly (lesson learnt from 'Shiny Sheff'.)

As we sailed closer to the Islands, we were continually being worked up to ensure that we would be ready for whatever was going to be thrown at us by the Argentines.

There was no doubt about it, we were at war and we needed to be as alert and practised as possible. We had to be at our best to fight and survive.

The Anti-Submarine and Anti-Air ships were very jumpy or very alert! Lots of spurious contacts were being reported. Some turned out to be real contacts, like our friend the 707, and an unknown Hercules. The force managed to identify it as ours by using the proper protocols for checking friend or foe.

The warmth of the Equator and Ascension was long forgotten; we were getting closer to the Antarctic Circle. We were in full arctic weather clothing; big white woollen seamen polo jumpers, white woolly socks rolled over arctic sea boots, waterproof jackets, black woollen balaclavas, which we would roll up to be woolly hats to look cool, and now our anti-flash gloves and hoods. Unfortunately, when the Sheffield was hit, they were in normal Defence Watches and not at Action Stations.

We were issued with white cotton 'Anti-flash' balaclavas and gloves, which were supposed to protect our hands and heads in case of fire. It was discovered that many of those injured on the Sheffield were not wearing their anti-flash when she was hit. The Command, quickly learnt lessons from the Sheffield disaster and this was one of them. It also helped by giving us some extra insulation out on the upper deck.

Tue 18th
Joined Hermes & Brilliant, feel safer now with air cover & Sea Wolf. Should have exercise Action Stns @ 10:45 but at 10:35 Air Raid Warning Yellow sounded indicating enemy aircraft within 100 miles, 2 minutes later Air Raid Warning Red - aircraft within 60 miles so real Action Stns, adrenalin really flowed. Turned out to be friendly so secured from Action Stations at 11:10 went for breakfast, just finished my cup of tea when

at 11:30 without prior warning Air Raid Warning Red; yet again Action Stns, but yet again friendly A/C. More ships joined or rather appeared on horizon including Coventry. 2 fires reported on board one on GDP (Gun Direction Position), but it turned out to be steam as they'd just switched the steam heating on in the bridge, the second a bit later on was actually a real one, but not all that big & was dealt with quickly. Nutty run out.

This was the day that we met the Task Force. We had escorts of Type 21 frigates for the transit to, and onwards from, Ascension, with their 4.5 radar-controlled guns, which were pretty effective at taking out targets, but the guns' reactions were not that fast and not the best weapon to deal with multiple aircraft. With Harriers and ships with Sea Dart and Sea Wolf we had a pretty effective safety net above and around us, and this knowledge gave me a better sense of security and wellbeing.

The aircraft warnings were coming from the AAW ships – Coventry etc., and we responded in kind by our reactions to get into the right positions around the ship to fight the enemy. It was a really exciting couple of hours, and very nerve-wracking.

There were also intelligence reports that Argentina had warned of massive air attacks against the Task Force to prevent us from landing in the Falkland Islands. The command were taking no chances and we were on high alert. From this day on, we had to carry our once only survival suits, AGR (gas masks) and wear our anti – flash all day. We were thousands of miles out at sea, just like the Belgrano and Sheffield were when they got hit and sunk. These incidents were playing on my mind all the way through this transit. We had plenty of protection around us and, as we were generally the centre of any screen (formation of ships), it was more than probable that another ship would take the hits for us. It didn't stop me from worrying though!

14

The Curse of The Albatross

Wed 19th

Still outside the TEZ, no Action Stations, but plenty of cross decking from Canberra to us; they transferred 40 Cdo to us and now we have 1500 men on board. Atlantic Conveyor rendezvoused with Invincible to transfer the Harriers, she also gave some to Hermes. Food cut down, all we had for dinner was 1 pasty & a cup of soup & a piece of bread. Doing another RAS with Tidepool. 1 Sea King from Hermes has ditched 22:40 7 survivors picked up so far (22:46) there were twenty nine men on board of which only 7 were picked up. The helo split as it hit the water and sunk almost instantly, the pilot survived & said all he heard was a loud bang & the next thing he knew he was in the water. It is believed to have been an Albatross flying into the tail rotors.
(Insert LCU's in South Atlantic Photo)

This was a really hectic day for every part of the Task Force. The Atlantic Conveyor had joined up with the main Task Force, and began distributing her load of Harriers to add to the main Harrier force. These were mainly GR3 (Ground Attack) RAF Harriers, that had not been tcstcd at sea. The additional RAF pilots really did have to learn very quickly how to land onto a moving deck. The target landing area on a grey ship, hidden on the horizon between sky and sea, in thousands of miles of dark ocean is a tiny spec compared to miles of airfield that they were used to! Fortunately, the weather on this day, although grey and murky with reduced visibility and low cloud, was not very windy, and the surface swell was low, so the ships were not rolling too heavily.

In times of war, risks are taken that would not be in peace time; cross decking troops in the middle of an ocean is one of them. This would generally be done in sheltered waters so that when we lowered the stern gate and allowed the water to flow into the ship to create a floating dock we reduced the risk of waves rushing into the ship and swamping the tank deck. In the conditions we were facing, the best we could do was to turn the ship in such a way that the waves would be crashing against the opposite side of the ship thus creating relative calm on the other side. Whilst it helped, doing much to protect those involved, it was still dangerous and would normally carry unacceptably high risk. We and the Canberra stayed fairly close to reduce the distance the landing craft had to sail between ships. There were a large number of people involved with the smaller landing craft, the crews in the Loading Dock and on the Davits that lowered the LCVPs and not to mention the Royal Marines, who had to climb down rope ladders with their full kit into the small landing craft rising up and down over 6ft swells and waves against the side of the ship. Nevertheless, we achieved it, and there was a steady flow of craft in and out of the floating dock at the back of the ship.

When the cross decking was complete, we had 465 Royal Marines from 40 Commando taking our total of men onboard to 2000! This was far in excess of what we designed to carry.

It took hours for the cross decking to be completed and, sadly, the day was not to end without disaster.

During one of the aircraft sorties, a Sea King carrying 29 SAS soldiers had a suspected bird strike and hit the water, turning over immediately and trapping a majority of the troops inside as it sunk to the bottom of the ocean.

The helicopter was heavily overloaded, I do not know why, but it would appear that the SAS, whose motto is Who Dares Wins, were daring to take the biggest risks and speed up the process. Sadly twenty one men lost their lives, including Corporal (Doc) Love RM DSM of 846 NAS. 846 Naval Air Squadron (NAS) are the Royal Marines helicopter wing (Junglys) and were our embarked NAS and were very much part of the ships company. During the South Georgia Operation, the SAS were advised not to land on the Fortuna Glacier but their CO refused to listen and insisted this was the best place for the troops to carry out their recce and advance from. We lost 2 Wessex helicopters and very nearly a third who went in to rescue the original crew, the rescue helicopter and the SAS troop. We have to be grateful that, at that time, we did not lose any men, but I believe many of those men that survived the Fortuna Glacier probably lost their lives later in another pointless exercise. They were not to blame for the bird strike, but the load in the aircraft must have had an effect on the flying.

The loss of these men had a massive effect on our morale. We had already lost shipmates on the Sheffield, 2 Harriers had collided in mid-air and the pilots were missing presumed dead and now twenty one of our very best had just died.

102

Not to diminish the loss the life, another disaster had befallen us. The day before, our 'nutty' supply had run out! You need to understand the importance of 'nutty' to a Matelot. It is what keeps the fleet afloat (and masking tape of course!) and if a Matelot cannot get his daily sweets and chocolate bar fix, life can be hell! It is one of the reasons we have the NAAFI 'Can Man' on board, the other being beer issue.!

Due to the need for more storage and priority supplies, we could not keep a full NAAFI and therefore our sweet supplies ran out! The 'Red Cross' parcels that were being sent out to the fleet were a godsend. Although the majority went to the Invincible Task Group, they did eventually get to us and it made for a happier crew.

Then to top it all, our scran was then being rationed! To an 18-year-old this was a real shock to the system. It was delivered around the ship in urns and on trays of hot piping pasties – read cool mini pasties! The soup was powdered but hot, the bread was fresh and baked in the galley.

We were not able to have fried food like chips, battered fish etc., because the galley was secured for action, and it would not have been sensible having boiling hot fat on the go whilst the ship was under attack. We still had fruit; Nelson introduced limes to his sailors to reduce scurvy and it was still important that we had a fresh supply at all times.

In the evening, we were served 'pot mess', a hot steaming stew, made up of everything that could be put in – meat (don't ask), potatoes, vegetables and whatever else the cooks saw fit to put in – it was delicious!

Breakfast became a bacon or sausage roll for a while, but thankfully, that returned to almost normal as we got used to the timings of the attacks and scheduled our lives around them.

Thurs 20th

Entered TEZ at 10:00ish when we went to Action Stations and we have remained in them all day. At 11:30 we were 130 miles from Stanley. The weather has been good to us, even though it's been bad, with visibility down to 1/2 a mile at times & 4 miles at the most, cloud cover was only 300ft, and we were expecting air attacks if it was clear during daylight hours, but obviously they wouldn't come out in this weather, so now at 20:00 we still haven't been attacked & are now falling out of Action Stations, we are due to go in tomorrow morning.

The tension aboard had really built by this time. The fleet were sailing in silent mode. There was no noisy communication being transmitted to each other; voice circuits, telephony and radar were all shut down.

Every manoeuvre that was made was signalled by flag, as in the days of Nelson, or by flashing light.

Each signal that was hoisted by the Command ship was repeated along the lines astern and abeam. Just before the signal was executed, the hoist was wiggled, and a minute later hauled down. This was repeated with all the ships in the formation, and all the ships manoeuvring, at almost exactly the same time; this was what being a signalman was all about. As exciting and exhilarating as it was to see it all working so well, there was still the fear that we would get attacked by air or Exocet missile.

We knew what had happened to our shipmates on the Sheffield and we had a mixture of emotions about it from outrage to the obvious fear that it could be us next.

The one shining light was that there was no sun shining. The sea was slightly choppy; it was wet, misty and murky. The sky and sea were almost as one and at times the cloud cover was low enough to cover the top of our mast. This added to the atmosphere and surreal image of a fleet at war; looking out across the sea, I could see a huge armada all around us. It was an impressive and awe inspiring sight, sailing into battle just as our predecessors had done and the films such as In Which We Serve demonstrated so well; it really was like an old black and white film, due to the clouds being so grey, so low and the damp adding to the grainy visage. But what an image and what a fleet! If I had been an Argentine spotter seeing what was coming towards me, I would have run like hell!

It always amazed me how we managed to get so many ships so close to shore during D-Day in June 1944; now it was my turn to experience this, with the knowledge that what we were about to do was perhaps even more dangerous because of the geography of the Islands and the narrow waterways we had to sail through to get to our D-Day anchorage. The Captain, as a submariner, was invited by the Commodore to work with Lt Cdr John Prime on anti-submarime measures for the Amphibious Force and overall deceptive measures, and the Captain was also given full control of the passage and anchorage for the amphibious force while the Commodore and Brigadier thought ahead for the landings and assault. Thus for the first hours of the final passage to San Carlos as the landing site, the force steered roughly for Port Stanley in case the Argentines should detect us: we knew they believed we would undertake the landings near our final objective. Then as darkness gathered we altered our base course westerly to pass well north of East Falkland, then turning south-south-west before finally south to make the entrance to Falkland Sound which divided the two main islands. The Captain sailed the ships as close to the West Falkland shore as he dared. This was because he was sure that if the entrance was mined, the mines would be in the middle of the channel. The Intrepid was not happy about this but war is all about taking the right sort of risks. In the event, the Argentines did not detect us at all until we entered Falkland Sound and started landing the Landing Force. In Max Hastings words this was "…arguably the most dangerous moment of the war…"

15

D - Day

Fri 21st

Just gone 23:59, visibility getting better, and weather improving making things difficult for us. Action Stns @ 01:30 getting head down for an hour. Arrived in Falkland Sound @ approx 03:30 and anchored. Air raid warning red sounded @ 04:15, and from 04:30 to 07:00 Argy positions were pounded relentlessly with NGS from Yarmouth and Antrim's 4.5 inch guns, then again at 08:30.

Closing down from Action Stations just hours before sailing so close to the Islands was a deliberate effort to enable everyone on board to get a bit of rest, some decent scran, and do what they had to do before they went to war. Captain Larken and his officers were brilliant at keeping morale up and made every effort to ensure we were looked after. I was on watch till 23:59, so could only try to crash out after I had handed over to Bill Byrne. The ship remained at Defence Watches (50% closed up).

We couldn't go below decks so we set up some sleeping space in the flag store by laying out a load of flags in their bags on the deck to make a mattress and half a dozen of us snuggled up in them to rest and keep warm, but sleep wouldn't come.

Most of the ship was already at Action Stations before the alarm sounded at 01:30; this was before we were in sight or sound of land though, with the air being so clear down South, I'm sure we could have been heard from ashore.

Having spent the whole day in low cloud, mist and rain; the weather as we approached the Islands started to clear. The cloud cover rose; it broke up and the stars became visible. The planning for the landings included darkness and part of the decision making was landing on a night when there was no moon, to reduce the risk of us all being seen. We were sailing in Falkland Sound between East and West Falklands; if you stood on a hill top looking over the Sound, you could have seen 20 plus ships sailing in single line between the Islands. I think this must have been our most vulnerable points of the war, but it was obvious and has been written that the Argentines were not expecting us to approach this way.

This had all been worked out on the Fearless, with Commodore Michael Clapp, Brigadier Julian Thompson RM, Major Ewen Southby-Tailyour RM, Captain Jeremy Larken and our Navigator Lt Cdr John Prime, amongst others. These men saved the lives of many Soldiers, Sailors and Airmen with their cunning and meticulous planning.

Major Southby-Tailyour had been in charge of the Royal Marines detachment in the Falklands during the 70s. He had navigated around the islands on a small yacht that he had shipped out and charted much of the waters that had not been charted before. His knowledge of the beaches, inlets and waterways was immense and, working as a team in the Command Room on board HMS Fearless, the Amphibious Command Team decided on the best place to carry out the landings, and best formations for the anchorages, to protect as many ships as possible from damage, destruction and loss of assets and lives.

As always, I was on the f'ocsle when it came to anchoring. We could hear the Naval Gunfire Support (NGS) pounding the positions ashore. There were a team of Argentine Special Forces on Fanning Head at the entrance to San Carlos Water and this was where a lot of the fire was going. We could also see tracer fire as our own Special Forces attacked the Argentine position. The noise of the ships engines, let alone the sound of the anchor chain clanging as it found its depth to secure the ship, negated any advantage we may have gained during our silent transit towards the Islands.

With all the noise and gunfire going on ashore, I became worried at how vulnerable we were, not as a ship but as individuals standing on the f'ocs'le. All it needed was a sniper with a night sight, and we could all have been popped off one by one. We were told to take cover behind the Bollards and Capstans as we dropped anchor, which was all well and good but just a few miles on the other side there could have been a whole load of other troops looking out for us – everybody within 10 miles must have heard the ships anchoring and there was no way anybody within 20 miles couldn't hear the Naval Gun Fire. We had certainly arrived in style!

At 06:30 the first wave of troops, 40 Cdo & 2nd Para went ashore and met no resistance. We weighed anchor & proceeded further inwards to San Carlos Water, I was on the Foc'sle and the Antrim & Yarmouth continued firing, there was gunfire ashore. SAS troops shot down a Pucara, Puma Chinook & a Canberra has been shot down. 45 Cdo & 3rd Para went ashore whilst we were weighing anchor.

We got through the original anchoring and the sailing into San Carlos with little or no bother. Yes, there had been plenty of noise from the guns and yes, we were closed up at Action Stations and our Gunners were ready with their World War II 40/60 Bofors and antiquated Sea Cat Missile system ready to take on the modern might of the supersonic Argentine Air Force, and positions ashore, but nothing happened!

We sailed in without a shot being fired at us by the Argentines, and without us firing a shot in anger. The weather was clear, calm and not too cold. The troops went ashore with no resistance. All the landing craft from the Fearless, Intrepid and the LSLs were busy picking up troops, holding a circular pattern until ordered to leave the ship's lee for shore. A lot of this was again done by flashing light with Aldis Lamps signalling to the Coxswain of the LCU or LCVP Command to beach.

I felt a mixture of excitement, anticipation, fear and sorrow for those men going ashore. Here I was 18 years old, sending signals by flashing light to order men to war and potentially their death. I was scared that I was now at war, but the unknown of what was going to happen was also adding to the excitement. I knew there was going to be further bloodshed, I knew that some of the men in the landing craft were not going to be coming back and I knew that we were going to be attacked at some point very soon. I didn't know how I would deal with it when it did happen; we had trained so hard for this day, from the day I joined up on 2nd June 1980 at 16½, the workups in Portland, war exercises in Norway, where we practised exactly this, in Arctic conditions, just in case we may at some point have to defend Northern Europe against the Russians, to the day we entered the TEZ and it was all for real; we could train no more. We had to wait and be counted when the time came.

I had an overwhelming need to be 'up top' if anything drastic happened to us. If we had to abandon ship, or the ship was damaged, I wanted to be out on the bridge wings so I could have space around me. I was determined to do my duty and serve my shipmates well, but not trapped inside. If the order came to abandon ship, I was afraid of having to fight my way blindly out of a burning wreck to survive. On the negative side, by being out in the open, I was also vulnerable to cannon and rocket fire from the aircraft; I had rationalised this by concluding that, should I be hit with any of this, it would probably kill me outright.

The closest we got to being hit during the initial operation in San Carlos was when a pattern of 3 x 6 inch shells from HMS Antrim gunfire support came towards us and we watched as first one, then two, on the Port side got closer and the third exploded just over the Starboard bow. A quick voice communication to their Ops room was sent, asking them very kindly to retarget!

16

Aircraft Green 30

Later on in the day it all started hotting up. We were attacked several times by Argy aircraft, mirage etc.., the planes were just coming over the tops of the hills diving down & dropping their bombs not really picking targets, non of the Amphib ships were hit. We opened fire with 40/60 & Sea Cat, which was practically useless because of the speed of the aircraft, although we had two near misses where the Sea Cat nearly found its target, one was fired ahead of the A/C & was training in towards it when the pilot obviously saw it & swung away narrowly missing destruction. The second near miss was virtually the same, the attacks came in waves of 3 or 4 a/c @ a time of which 2 or 3 were destroyed in every attack, although we didn't get any. Intrepid fired the first Sea Cat in the first attack at a Canberra bomber, but it was wasted, it narrowly missed S.S. Canberra, shot passed us as the A/C flew very low & close to us, & the Sea Cat just exploded in the side of the hills. We have nine Rapier (Anti-Air) batteries (courtesy of T Bty 12 Regt AA Det RA) which were supposed to have been set up by first light but were not ready for use until nearly dusk by which time the air attacks had stopped, but maybe they'll be of use tomorrow. Five of our ships were hit, 2 badly damaged with Ardent being destroyed & 20 blokes left dead, Argonaut was hit astern by a 500lb bomb, as she was patrolling the entrance to our anchorage, and she now has two 500lb unexploded bombs inside her. I don't know yet of her casualties. Broadsword was hit by machine guns from the a/c & suffered splinter damage from 2 bombs which exploded near to her, knocking out her Sea Wolf & Exocet missile systems & sonar, so she's useless now. Antrim was hit astern but the bomb didn't explode, and was diffused by disposal experts. Brilliant was damaged, but not seriously. Argonaut cannot move. SHAR arrived late on the scene but there was great improvement in air defence when they did, with them shooting down 8. Altogether 17 A/C were shot down.

We knew at some point an attack on us was imminent. The first sign was when a Pucara ground attack aircraft popped out over the top of the hills to the North. It was almost skimming the ground and following the contours of the land. The pilot must have had a bigger shock than we did when we saw the lone aircraft, and he suddenly came across more than twenty warships, with thousands of trigger-happy Matelots waiting for you! All on the GDP and Bridge Wings heard the aircraft, I caught sight of it and along with many other voices screamed "Aircraft green three zero" and pointing in the direction of the aircraft. The whole of San Carlos erupted in gun and missile fire as all the ships in the vicinity opened up on him. The pilot banked sharply right, I imagine with several expletives and fuelled by adrenalin, and did a 180 degree turn to scarper back over the top to safety! We now knew how we would react and the surge of adrenalin-fuelled energy was palpable. It wouldn't be long now before the next attacks would happen, as there was no doubt this startled pilot was reporting back to the mainland what he had just encountered.

The only personal weapons I had to fight the Argentine Air Force were my eyes, reinforced with binoculars and voice. The ship's armaments had been reinforced with GPMGs mounted along the various decks and manned mainly by Royal Marines. Others who had weapons (including the SAS who resided on our Port signal deck) lined the ship's sides to join in the 'firefights'.

During the transit south, the Chief Yeoman (Mick Tapping) asked me to volunteer for the GPMG, which was to be mounted on the GDP on the Bridge roof, bang in the centre and open to the world. I didn't say no but I was terrified about being so exposed, even with a weapon. Why he wanted me to do it I'll never know, but I didn't feel I refused the request and, in a small way, I felt quite proud to have been chosen. These were all very contradictory thoughts but, at 18, my emotions were up and down like a yo-yo. My Dad's words, "Now's your chance son. Your chance to do your bit!" were with me when I said 'yes'.

However, my fears about the appointment, as well as worries about whether I should have said 'no' were soon relieved.

It didn't take long for word to get around the Comms department that I was to be the 'Gimpy' on the GDP. Some of the young Royal Marine Comms detachment that worked with us were rather hacked off that a Matelot had been given the chance to fire a gun at the enemy and not them. In fact one was very vocal and demanded to know "Why is a f*****g Skate being given a gun? We're trained to kill, not that lot of ponces." The Chief Yeoman called me over and discussed this with me. He wanted to know if I would be disappointed if I handed the' Gimpy' over to the "Baby Royal."

"Oh Chief! If they feel that strongly about it let them have it. I'm sure I'll get over it." and there it was, gone; along with any guilt I may have felt about not doing my bit!

About an hour after the Pucara incident, Air Raid Warning Red was called and all the ship's sirens blasted out to ensure all other ships knew what was coming. This became a very eerie and portent sound as the days went on.

The ship was silent, the ships in the anchorage were silent and still with all eyes, binoculars and guns pointing towards the direction of the threat, generally to Fanning Head at the mouth of San Carlos Water. Our frigates were patrolling in and around the anchorage, one posted at the entrance, another out in Falkland Sound to warn us and also try to take out some aircraft before they got through. Their primary role was to protect the amphibious ships in any way they could, and some did at the ultimate price.

We were promised air cover by the Sea Harriers from the Carrier Group to fly CAP some seventy five plus miles north-west, out in the stormy South Atlantic. We also had Rapier Anti-Air Missile batteries set up on top of the mountains surrounding San Carlos to take out the aircraft, which provided reassurance from day one that we were well covered.

The first waves of aircraft came screaming into San Carlos Water and Dante's Inferno was opened up. The Argentines sent everything they had out to us – Mirage, Skyhawks and British Canberras. They came at mast and bridge height, flying low from the mainland to avoid detection and, like the Pucara on the first Pathfinder mission, just popped over the tops of the mountains. This time, they didn't turn and run. They only had seconds to choose a target due to the way the Amphibious Command Team and genius of our Navigator Lt Cdr John Prime laid out the ships to anchor. But they didn't waste any of those seconds! As soon as they were in the anchorage, they opened up with 20 mm cannon and rockets, they dropped 500 and 1,000 British made bombs in the general direction of the ships. Every ship in the water opened up with everything they had.

HMS Intrepid fired the first missile, letting a Sea Cat loose at a Canberra (the aircraft not our P&O Liner used for carrying troops); it went rogue, just missing the arse end of S.S. Canberra, flying just in front of our bow and exploding into the hillside. Although we were a team, there was a lot of rivalry between us and the Intrepid, and we were not too impressed by their actions. We were to get our own back so to speak when, during another attack, the same thing happened to one of our Sea Cats going in their direction, and, rather too close for comfort, it clipped the life raft of one of the Intrepid's LCUs as it was reversing out of their tank deck. Thankfully the missile crashed harmlessly into the sea. Obviously not a deliberate act but it 'evened the score', and prevented any unhealthy gloating on our part!

The Sea Cat Missile system was designed in the 60s for much slower aircraft and was totally impotent against the speed of the Mirages and Skyhawks. Our aimers quickly worked this out and began tracking the aircraft and aiming just in front of their flight paths, some got close, but the pilots were quick to react. The missiles were loaded with chains and shrapnel and could be detonated before impact and some missiles were exploded near to an aircraft in the hope that the shrapnel would take them out, but this never really worked. It was amazing to watch the track of the missile aiming at an aircraft as I described above. Watching it flying directly at a plane expecting it to impact and take it out. Claims were made by some ships that their Sea Cat attacks had been successful, but I never saw one on the Fearless.

Throughout the day, we were attacked several times. Sometimes by sixteen plus aircraft at a time; always coming in formations of 3 or 4. The noise was intense; the screaming of the aircraft as they flew past a few feet above our heads, the noise of their cannon fire and rockets being launched at the ships, the 'thud, thud, thud, thud' of the Bofors as they fired their clips of 40/60 shells at the planes, the 'whoosh' and smoke of the Sea Cat being launched not twenty feet away from where we were standing, the smell of cordite burning the nostrils, the shouting from the lads and on the intercom when planes were spotted and the small arms fire from all around the ship. It was utterly terrifying and totally exhilarating all at once. There was too much going on around you to worry about being scared and it wasn't until the lull after an attack that the fear really kicked in as we had little time to consider what might have been. There wasn't long to ponder on it though, as it was only thirty minutes to an hour before the next wave of aircraft came in. At the end of an attack, the ship's sirens sounded, the ship went silent and we stared; we didn't talk, we waited, and then, BANG, it would all start again.

The Argentine pilots were totally mad! Some were flying at less than fifty ft above the water, firing their cannons at us and just before dropping their bombs they would pull up and the bombs would fly in towards the ships. At times they were so close you could see the pilot's face. Crazy but skilful and brave flying!

One of the most difficult aspects of the day was that we had not had any air cover during the attacks. There had been a lot of animosity amongst the Amphibious Group and the Carrier Group throughout the transit south. The news reports only ever mentioned the Hermes and Invincible; they were the glory ships and it wound the rest of us up no end. One of the many nicknames we gave to the Hermes and her force was 'FOSA' (Flag Officer South Africa) because they were that far East of the Islands. This meant that the Harriers on patrol only had a short time on station, and it seemed every time they handed over we had an air attack and very little, if any, cover to take out the Argentinian Air Force. Admiral Sandy Woodward onboard the Hermes had to ensure that we kept the carriers safe. If one of them was taken out by an Excocet missile or other attack then we would not have been able to fight the war so effectively, if indeed at all. Whilst we moaned about it, I think most of us recognised and accepted the reasons.

When the Harriers did come into contact, they were incredibly effective and did an amazing job in diminishing the Argentine Air Force capability. The 'political' infighting amongst the senior Command is clearly highlighted in Amphibious Assault Falklands, Michael Clapp and Ewen Southby - Tailyour, but it really did come to a head on the first day of the landings. The anger amongst all of us including senior officers was plain to see and hear at the lack of air cover we received. The Rapier had never been tested at sea, and after such a long transit, with its sensitive electronics, it took time to settle down and would not be ready for at least twenty four hours after being set up – this was unknown at the time.

What was known was when an attack was launched from the mainland and how many aircraft were coming to get us. We had people on the ground in Argentina, reporting the activity. They were approximately 340 miles away, our Harriers less than 100 but, on day one, they were not on station during the first attacks. They arrived late or they attacked the Argentines as they were leaving 'Bomb Alley', as San Carlos was soon to be known, not before they arrived. This left us vulnerable and the damage to the fleet on that day was dramatic, with 5 ships being hit. The Harriers, when in action, were an amazing piece of kit and our pilots did a brilliant job in destroying the Argentine Air Force, but, for us, it always felt that they were too late and we suffered much because of the lack of cover provided.

HMS Ardent, the Type 21 Frigate, was attacked out in the Sound, taking 8 bombs and losing power; she was lost to us after putting up a brave fight. The little Frigate HMS Yarmouth went out to pick up survivors. She pulled up alongside Ardent's bow as her stern had been ripped apart by all the explosions and the survivors stepped off and on to the safety of this brave little ship. Yarmouth was also there for the Sheffield when she was hit and was towing her before she sank. Her Captain must have been something else and her crew were brilliant.

HMS Broadsword was also hit out in the Sound; her Sea Wolf (CIWS) was taken out as well as her Exocet missile system. The Sea Wolf was a very modern CIWS and worked brilliantly on many occasions, taking out many aircraft during the war, but for a day or two she was useless to us as a fighting unit. Her radars worked which were Anti-Air, which were of use, but she had no defensive systems.

HMS Argonaut was patrolling the entrance of 'Bomb Alley' with very little difference in armament than ours, 2 x quadruple Sea Cat Launchers and 2 x 40/60 Bofors. The difference with Argonaut was that she had been refitted in 1980 and had Exocet missiles fitted. These were great for surface warfare but not against aircraft. She was hit by two 500lb bombs, which didn't explode; they did damage her steering gear and engines, and she couldn't move, and the bombs were diffused by Staff Sargeant Jim Prescott and Warrant Officer John Phillips.

HMS Antrim, a County Class Destroyer, was heavily armed with twin gun turret 4.5 inch guns, Exocet Missiles, Sea Slug (SAM) and good old Sea Cat, but also took a 1,000lb Bomb which came in through the Sea Slug launcher and settled itself in the aft toilets. This was also removed by the FCDT; I remember quite clearly seeing the tangled wreck of the missile launcher as she anchored at the back of San Carlos before they began the long and arduous task of removing the bomb.

HMS Brilliant, another Type 22 like the Broadsword, suffered minor splinter damage during the attacks, but nothing serious.

The miracle of this day was that none of the amphibious ships was badly hit. The Frigates and Destroyers had done their job protecting us at great cost. That was their role and they did it brilliantly.

Whilst I refer to it as a 'miracle', Lt Cdr John Prime, explained the reasons for choosing San Carlos and why the anchorage was laid out as it was. 'Apart from other tactical reasons, San Carlos Water had been selected for the Amphibious Task Force anchorage after lessons learnt at our own Captain's behest during exercises in the Norwegian Fjords. The aim in San Carlos was to get the amphibious ships to anchor close in to shore under the limited but useful cover of the surrounding hills, whilst our heroic guardian frigates and destroyers stood guard in the entrance. COMAW had asked for and received an RAF Buccaneer pilot to join his staff and Fl Lt White duly arrived at Ascension with his kit lost back in the UK. John Prime asked him to draw flight paths and timings on the anchorage chart that attacking bombers would most likely take to approach and enter San Carlos, identify their target and release their bombs. Provided with this information, the ships were directed to anchor in positions clear of these paths and use their engines to maintain navigation safety as well as A Arcs for whatever armament they had.

The result was that apart from a particular adventurous duo who flew in from Sussex mountains in the south and put unexploded bombs in Galahad and Lancelot, no amphibious shipping took a direct hit. The time in the target area was less than 8 secs, making selection of target and release of weapon at very low height very difficult.

This was not luck as so many have proclaimed but the result of good tactical planning.'

17

Say A Little Prayer

We lost 2 Gazelle helos, and a pilot of one of them was machine gunned down by the Argies as he swam ashore. There has been heavy fighting ashore but I don't know much about that, but NGS carried on throughout the day. I didn't get any sleep and had been awake and on the signal deck from 20:00 the night before. We were secured at 21:00 today & are allowed to get our heads down till 03:00, when we come on watch till 09:00. Scrans still only a mug of pot mess & a roll (even breakfast!) and during the day we get hot soup and for an 'Action snack' we get a pasty & an apple!

We were all to get an idea of how the Argentines would behave in battle and it was not going to be in line with the Geneva Convention.

Whilst one of the AAC Gazelles was doing a recce it came under fire from Argentine troops ashore. The chopper was hit and went down into shallow water. The pilot was killed, but the navigator survived the crash and, as he was swimming towards the shore, the Argentinians opened up on him and gunned him down. This was witnessed by our own troops and created a massive moral outrage. It was the sort of thing we were bought up on as children, watching films of the Second World War and the 'filthy Hun' cowardly shooting down our Paras as they got stuck in trees, or airman trying to climb out of crashed aircraft. It shouldn't happen. He should have been taken as a prisoner of war; but what did we really expect when after the reports we had received of the Military Junta torturing, killing or disappearing tens of thousands of their own people that talked out or protested against them? We knew we were going to be fighting a dirty war and it couldn't have made the lads ashore feel any better about their chances if they were captured. I'm sure knowing the way our lads' minds worked, they were determined to get revenge for this act of murder and ensure his death would not be in vain; just as we knew when HMS Sheffield was hit, we were not going to let them get away with it.

At the end of the day, when we were secured from Action Stations, those that could went down to get some 'scran' and grab some kip. There was a real buzz about the ship, with everybody talking about how exciting the day had been, what they'd seen, how we'd 'done the Argies', and other dits. It was exciting and talking about it and laughing and joking with the lads over a tinnie in the mess, it took my mind off how I really felt.

I decided I needed a trip to the 'heads' and stepped out of my mess to find a queue! I knew we had a few extra souls on board, but I had never witnessed this before, even ashore - it was only the ladies who had to queue. Eventually I got my go but as I was preparing to leave and get back to get some rest, my whole body started shaking, from my feet right up to my head. It was weird and I couldn't control it. I sat there for about five minutes trying to regain control, and I started to pray, really pray:

"Dear God, Please help me to get through this. Please support me and my shipmates and help us all to get home safely. Amen."

It wasn't until after I said this prayer that I stopped shaking. I have always had a belief in God; I may not go to church every Sunday, but I have always believed in a higher being. At this time, he was the most important thing in the world to me, and the only thing I could think of. I was scared and needed help. This little bit of spirituality bought me back to reality. This must have been the effect of a combination of the shock of the attacks and the adrenalin finally releasing itself from my body. I felt better afterwards and guessed that this was the reason why there was such a queue for the heads. There was very little other privacy on board.

18

Lull in The Proceedings

Sat 22nd

Had a good four hours sleep during the night, and am now fairly wide awake. Gun bombardment been going on all night in the area of Goose Green. It's 06:00 and all quiet. Not much happened today & there were no attacks though one was building up 80 miles north of us at about 20:00 but they just circled the area for an hour then turned back. A Harrier sank an F.P.B. or rather beached it and left it burning.

I was really desperate for sleep! The last 48 hours had been hectic with the terror and excitement of the air attacks throughout the day; the horrendous spectacle of ships burning, planes exploding around us and crashing into the hillsides and the horror stories of downed British Helicopter pilots being murdered as they tried to swim ashore. I climbed onto my pit fully clothed and I was gone. I had not been below decks in my pit since the 19th when we entered the TEZ, and I was knackered. I felt a lot more secure and comfortable than the Royals, Paras and Pongos that had to dig in on the hillsides around us. The Argentines had limited night flying capabilities with their British built Canberra aircraft. In later discussions with Captain Larken, he stated 'I personally was nervous that they might try high-level bombing along the line of closely packed LSLs and STUFT as observed by the attacking aircraft during the day; that was why ships always moved from their daytime anchorages (designed to make life difficult relative to the observed 'flylines' the daytime attackers were obliged to fly relative to the hills etc... each night). The soldiers on the hillsides not only had to put up with the cold and damp, but be aware and alert at all times in case of incursion by enemy troops.

Even though we were miles away, we could hear the naval gunfire as Goose Green was being pounded. I have never been on the end of an artillery bombardment, but it sounded terrible. The enemy troops on the receiving end had probably not even been aware that we had arrived, and then to be suddenly pounded from out of nowhere, must have been both shocking and terrifying. Artillery bombardments have been used effectively throughout the history of warfare, certainly in the 1st World War, 2nd World War and Aden. They are used to weaken the resolve of the enemy troops, so when the time for hand-to-hand fighting actually comes, they are in no fit state physically or mentally to respond. The most well-known results of these bombardments, is 'bomb happy' that came from the reactions of the British troops from the 1st and 2nd World Wars, some who couldn't function properly on their return. Today we know it as PTSD (Post Traumatic Stress Disorder).

I'm not sure why we weren't attacked by air on this day. The Argentinians could really have pressed home an advantage after the first day but it was quiet and we hoped they were licking their wounds after the battering their air force had suffered at the hands of our Task Force and Harriers. In reality, we knew it was likely the high Command were reconfiguring their air force units and spreading the remaining planes around to create the illusion that they were in control of the air. We were at Action Stations from 1st light to sunset and were warned of a large attack forming but this never came. There was an eerie and tense silence throughout the day as we waited and watched, waited and watched; this is how it was for any air raid warning. The ship's sirens sounded and the whole of the upper deck went silent. The helicopters would scatter and land wherever they could on the shore/hillside for camouflage and protection. All eyes were on Fanning Head, waiting to see the first aircraft come through the gap, or on the hills left and right of us. Our eyes scanning slowly through our binoculars, looking for aircraft or vapour trails higher up, althought usually it turned out that these were Harriers. After a long day of waiting, nothing had happened. I was relieved, but also worried about what was to come the next day.

A couple of Harriers, that were actually on CAP, came across a small patrol boat in one of the inlets and identified it as Argentinian. They swooped down, and fired on it with rockets and cannon fire. The boat took flight and steered towards shore. The Captain of the boat grounded the ship and the crew escaped. The Harriers felt they had done enough and didn't finish the boat off as it was burning away. It transpired that the boat was carrying a couple of light artillery pieces that survived the attack and were later recovered by the Argentinians and used against our troops. These were difficult calls to make and, as I reflect, I am proud that we operated in an honourable way, allowing the crew to escape; the Harrier pilots had a lot of pressure on them as we all did and they took the decisions that they felt were right.

19

HMS Antelope

Sun 23rd

Action all round today with air attacks late in the afternoon @ about 16:00, with a wave of four coming in first & not going out again. There were 10 planes altogether that attacked us & 2 that were going to but were attacked by Harriers over Pebble Island, one got shot down & the other jettisoned its load & legged it being chased by Harriers, but they didn't need to do anything to it because it got into difficulties & smashed into the sea. The others - 2 were got by Antelope but only after she received 2 bombs that didn't explode on impact but later on, & I'll come to that in a minute. 1 of the planes hit Antelope's main mast & bent it to a 90 degree angle then crashed into the sea, another was hit by Antelope's Sea Cat & it exploded into pieces right in front of our eyes one minute it was there & the next 'BADOOSH' gone! It looked really spectacular!

Plymouth got 2 as well I think - 1 with her Oerlikon 20 mm cannon & one with Sea Cat. Rapier claimed 2. We nearly had 1 with a 40/60 & Sea Cat but the 40/60 had to stop firing for fear of hitting the Rapier Bty on top of the hill, but if he had a bit more time he would have got it, & the Sea Cat was almost right on it when yet again the plane out manoeuvred it, flew straight over a Rapier Battery & was blown out of the sky! Moral of this story is - never fly over a Rapier Bty when being chased by a Sea Cat! There were missiles flying around everywhere & Intrepid was narrowly missed by a Sea Cat supposedly from us but we only fired 2 & Rapier missiles were all above us exploded everywhere, one exploded a couple of hundred yds off our Port side & one narrowly missed the Fo'c'sle.

The other four; I'm not sure who got them but someone did. Harriers shot 1 down over Pebble Island & chased another away making it jettison its load & it later ditched into the sea. We also got 2 Puma's or rather troops ashore did. But unfortunately we lost a Harrier.

Well back to the Antelope. It was 21:20 & we had just fallen out from Action Stations feeling really chuffed, when all of a sudden there was a big white flash. I turned round just in time to see a huge ball of flame & bits of metal flying everywhere, they were detonating the bomb & it had just exploded. Within 1/2 an hour half the ship was ablaze & burning fiercely & out of control. Within seconds of the explosion, there were helos on the spot, one had just landed on an LSL seconds before & illuminated Antelope instantly, if the helo had been in the air 30 seconds earlier another helo would have been lost. Black smoke was everywhere & at times we couldn't see the flames or the ship. Plymouth was at the scene in a few minutes to take off survivors & all our LCUs & LCVPs were there & took them off. By this time you could see the inside of the ship as there was a gaping hole in its stbd side. The ships company were all mustered on the flight deck in their once only suits & @

21:52 we got the last message from the RO on the bridge saying 'Some ships company are cut off from getting aft. Am abandoning ship to Port'

Then about 23:00, there was another flash & muffled explosion as its boilers went up, it continued burning through furiously and at 23:35 there was yet another explosion larger, louder & more dazzling than the first with pieces of red hot, jagged metal being blasted high & far over a wide area as it's Sea Cat magazine went up, we on the upper deck had to take cover for fear of being hit. The ship burned on through the night & @ 04:00 its' 4.5 mag went up.

This was an incredible day. The noise was deafening, the attacks were manic in their ferocity and audacity of the pilots. Having experienced the first day, we thought we had an idea of what to expect when we were attacked but still nothing prepared us for the intensity of the day. We were getting continual commentary from the bridge, with either the Captain or Navigator keeping us updated on the reports and events of the day.

It was like a turkey shoot. There was tracer fire from small arms, Lieutenant Colonel Michael Rose of the SAS (who had led the Iranian Embassy siege rescue) sat in his deck chair on the Port signal deck with an array of weapons next to him and popped shots off, Bofors, 4.5 inch guns, missiles, aircraft all flew through the air. I was moving around on the signal deck from one bridge wing to another, trying to keep up with what was where, screaming out "AIRCRAFT! Green 10" etc… above the noise as another Skyhawk, Canberra or Mirage appeared over the top or through the gap, coming head on at us. It was a constant 'Douf, Douf, Douf' Douf, Douf' as the Bofors discharged their hail of fire. The loaders were working flat out, as the gunner pulled the trigger constantly, aiming up and down as his oppo tried to manually turn the gun as quickly as he could towards the next enemy attack.

As I mentioned previously, the Sea Cat Missile system was an antiquated piece of kit that was launched in the 60s. It was a wire-guided missile system, and targeted by sight and not radar. It consisted of 4 missiles manually loaded onto a launcher by a loading team. We had four on the Fearless and four on the Intrepid. Other ships including Antelope were fitted with this system – it was the weapon of choice on the older ships.

Fearless and Intrepid's launchers were 2 forward of the bridge and 2 aft, just before the flight deck. The aimers were in little capsules on top of the Bridge in the GDP (Gun Direction Platform) and two aft of the signal deck overlooking the missiles, as close as they could be. They were alerted of the threat generally by the communicators or Ops room crew, who received warnings of in coming aircraft, and then they steadied themselves on the bearing of the threat, hoping the course of the aircraft would remain true.

Obviously in such close quarters as San Carlos, the 'noise' on the radar plot quickly lost the aircraft and so the aimers had to rely on good old human eyes to seek their target. Essentially all fire control and weapon direction came from visual sightings from the GDP team and bridge wings. The age of the missile, meant it was designed for an earlier part of aviation history and, if all the Argentinians had to throw at us was our old Canberras and their Pucaras, we may have stood a chance, but against modern supersonic aircraft (even though they weren't flying at supersonic speeds when attacking us) it was almost laughable. However, with the Seacats in the air and the intense fire from everything else the ships in 'Bomb Alley' had to throw at the aircraft, the pilots were intimidated enough that it reduced their accuracy of fire and dropping their bombs on us.

The aimers were brilliant and I watched as one of our missiles was launched towards a jet, the pilot obviously caught sight of the missile and banked away to avoid being hit by the Sea Cat. The aimer followed it and chased it as far as he could. The aircraft screamed away from the missile putting a safe distance between itself and the Sea Cat. The Sea Cat has an early detonation option (manual of course) and, if detonated, dispatched hot molten chain and shrapnel to cause damage to any aircraft in its near vicinity, but the aimer couldn't use it on this occasion. He was so close to a hit with this attack, we were cheering him on, willing him to get it, but we watched mesmerised as the aircraft flew in the direction of a Rapier Battery (Royal Artillery surface to air missile system – wire-guided, but radar-controlled) and saw the Rapier launch and get a quick and direct hit of the aircraft. The explosion was as good as any you see in war films, and the wreck of the aircraft cascaded down on to the hillside. There wasn't much left of it and the pilot certainly did not get out. This may have been more luck than judgement or planned teamwork but, in the bigger picture, this is what teams are all about, working together, looking out for one and other. I realised 25 years after the war exactly what teamwork is and how we were all part of one great team.

Sadly, Rapier did not work on our first day. It didn't take too kindly to 8,000 miles of tossing about on the oceans. It was designed as an air defence system for use in Germany as part of the Cold War and the electronics inside were very sensitive. They took time to settle and I'm sure the lads from the Royal Artillery and RAF were as frustrated as we were. It was felt by many that the number of ships damaged on the 21st, was due to the absence of Rapier, as well as the Harriers being too far out to get the Argentines as they came in.

What it did prove though, was Rapier was a formidable weapon when working to its full capacity, and I know many of us were relieved to see it in action, once it was ready.

The Sea Cat could also be unpredictable and a few went 'rogue' (lost control), including the one that nearly hit the Intrepid on this day, apparently fired by us.

As I mentioned earlier, the frigates were there to protect us and HMS Antelope, with her 4.5 Gun and Sea Cat Missile systems, was using her gas turbine engines to full effect to weave in between the capital ships to provide cover. She took two bombs. One during an attack where her foremast aerial was bent at ninety degrees. This was another demonstration of the crazy approach taken by enemy pilots; on this occasion the aircraft was flown so low that the pilot, having released the bomb, couldn't pull up fast enough and crashed into the sea. Not long afterwards, another aircraft exploded in front of our eyes. I had just witnessed two people dying without really registering the fact. To me, they had crashed or exploded in spectacular fashion and were no longer a threat. I had nothing but excitement and celebration in me as I watched the plane explode further added to by the big cheer from all of us. It didn't matter that we had just witnessed the death of a human being, just that the Argentinians had one less plane or pilot to attack us with. Two days into the war and I had already become desensitised to death. I don't know whether I was focussed on the machines, rather than the person inside, or whether it was the group celebration, but I know I felt nothing for those pilots that I saw die on this day.

The Antelope steamed across our bows, almost in an act of defiance for any Argentines watching, as this tiny frigate demonstrated her mettle in battle; clearly showing her bent mast and the hole in the Port side, where the bomb entered the ship.

She was directed to what was considered a safe anchorage at the back end of San Carlos, away from other ships, so the EOD team could make the bomb safe.

We had secured from Action Stations, slightly later than normal due to the amount of activity being detected by other units further out to sea, or possibly on the mainland. I was walking around the wings, securing the signal deck, ensuring the halyards were tight and not flapping in the wind, the 10 and 20 inches were facing in the correct direction, the Aldis Lamps were secured in their boxes and the flag lockers were closed down and the flap secured. Doing all this may sound pointless to people amidst the chaos of active combat but the routines that kept things normal and maintained standards on board, are part of what makes our military so formidable. It was also very calming routine work that gave me a measure of choice and control.

Our part of the ship always had to be stowed away correctly. There is nothing worse being on the upper scupper, in a light breeze and hearing the halyards rattling in the wind! They had to be secured tightly on the cleats. There was a way of doing it, which I was taught by CY Moutter, and that is what I did every night before I went below decks.

It was as I was securing the Starboard flag locker, I was bending down, facing towards the Port side and winding the rope around the cleats, when suddenly there was a huge bang; it was deafening and was accompanied by a great white flash as I looked up. As we looked over to our Starboard side, a massive fire ball shot into the sky "Oh God No!" all the lads on the Starboard wing that night said in unison. I looked over in horror at the ship burning. I could see the ship's company standing on the flight deck in their orange once only suits. They were illuminated by the flames that roared out of a gigantic hole in the Port side.

My first thoughts were of the Bomb Disposal soldier that was attempting to detonate the bomb. I knew that he was dead. There really could not have been much left of him, after such a blast. I pictured him in my mind, leaning over the bomb, slowly, carefully unscrewing the detonator, and I hoped with everything in me that he didn't feel anything or know anything when the bomb exploded. We found out later, that Staff Sergeant Jim Prescott Conspicuous Gallantry Medal posthumous was killed by the blast, and his oppo, Warrant Officer John Phillips lost an arm. John was in another compartment and when the bomb exploded it took the door off, and the clips that secured the door, were blown off and one took his arm off at the shoulder. John later explained that Staff Sergeant Jim Prescott was killed by the door hitting him square on and, in death, he looked the same without any injury. His body was never recovered and fittingly went down with the ship. I hope this is the truth for Jim's family's sake but, to this day, I cannot get out of my head the image of his body being ripped apart by the explosion of a thousand pound bomb, whilst he was leaning over it, trying to save one of our ships and the crew on board.

I watched horrified and mesmerised at the ship burning fiercely. As soon as the blast happened, helos were straight on the scene, illuminating the crew and starting to lift them off. One of our LCVPs, commanded by Coxswain Corporal Alan White, was alongside in minutes, to start unloading the crew and get them to the safety of HMS Fearless. Other landing craft from Fearless and Intrepid were quick to join in.

It was horrific, and all I could do was watch as a ship, not more than a thousand yards away, died.

I could see all the decks; I could see metal dripping into the sea; I could see the hole getting wider; I could see the crew, calmly climbing down the ship's side into landing craft or boats to be taken to safety. I was terrified. I saw at close hand what could happen to a ship and I couldn't take my eyes off it. Even when I was relieved so I could get some scran, it was the talk of the dining hall and I wanted to see more. I went back up top after eating to see what was going on. It was a morbid fascination. The helicopters were still hovering over the ship, and illuminating the fire-fighting crews that had come from other ships in the bay, as well as Antelope's own.

It was no good, there was nothing that could be done for her. The RO on watch on the bridge received a message from HMS Antelope, "Am cut off aft, abandoning ship forward!"

The RO had remained with the Captain to relay messages on his portable kit to keep the group updated. A boat was alongside to take them off. It was terrifying and heart breaking at the same time to hear those words, but a relief to watch them climb down a ladder on the ship's side into safety.

We watched her all through the night, having to take cover as her magazine exploded sending white hot metal flying out through the air and across the bay. The explosion was massive, bigger it seemed than the bomb exploding. I think this is the first time I 'hit the deck' (which was the position everybody below decks had to adopt during air attacks), to avoid the debris that we expected to come down on us. Fortunately, it never did, but I could not take my eyes off the poor ship whilst I was on watch through the night.

20

Wrecking the 40/60 Crews

Mon 24th

Antelope still burning & @ 10:00 she was just a smouldering wreck with a thick screen of smoke drifting across the bay.

10:30. Her back broke & her middle sunk leaving her bows & stern sticking up & slowly they are disappearing by tomorrow she should be gone.

Only 2 people were killed altogether, the first when the bomb actually hit the ship & went through ripping a Steward's head off & the second was the disposal bloke, with his mate losing an arm.

We were actually attacked for the first time today. They changed their tactics & attacked from behind giving them an 18 mile run down the valley & a clear view of all the ships. They were picked up on a voice circuit in the Ops & a Sub-Lieut. who can speak Spanish was called in & he said that their main target is Fearless & the LSLs apparently our name was said in English. The jets (Mirage & Skyhawk) came screaming down the valley in waves of 3 & 4 again flying very low about 10 or 20 ft above the water line, instantly dropping bombs & firing 20 mm cannon. Hitting RFA Sir Galahad going in but not exploding, she also received cannon fire &

rocket fire starting fires which were soon extinguished. RFA Sir Lancelot received an UXB as well. Then they turned on us opening up with 20mm cannon & rockets & bombs they came straight at us from ahead this time & were instantly opened up on with 40/60 which had been firing continuously, the 1 on the Port side actually getting a Mirage & Sea Cat which again almost had one but it chased the plane over a Rapier Bty & yet again they took it. The front of the bridge was strafed with cannon fire & 1 shell came straight through 1 10" signal lantern smashing the glass & shutters & knocking the back of it, some of the glass hit one of the supply numbers on the stbd gun on the wrist making him drop his clip of four shells, his hand getting covered in blood, his white anti-flash gloves changing colour instantly to red, & leaving the bridge wing covered in spots of blood & broken glass & bits of metal; the steel screen behind the 20" signal lantern now has hole in it where a 20 mm shell went through. The stbd bridge wing was now short of supply numbers, & I became one, as one of the gunners had shown me what to do days before in case one got hit so I could do the job. The Port gun lost 2 supply numbers 1 being hit in the foot, but fortunately he was wearing steel toe capped DMS boots & his foot or rather his toes were badly bruised & cut, he lost most of his toe nails though if it wasn't for the fact he was wearing steel toe caps, he would have lost his toes. The other lad got hit on the head & in the leg & he lost a lot of blood. He was hit & just collapsed on the deck, one of the blokes thought he had just fainted as he made no sound when he went down. A shell ripped through his leg sending blood & flesh everywhere, & one hit his steel helmet splitting it right across the top & splitting his head open & the steel dug into his skull; if he wasn't wearing his helmet he would more than likely be dead now, but as it is he is ashore having surgery on his leg. Another bloke on the stbd gun was saved by his helmet as a piece of shrapnel hit it on the back denting it & splitting it, he didn't realise he had been hit until someone pointed it out to him. A shell or rocket thudded into the sandbags on the bridge roof but didn't explode. A bomb was dropped very close to our stbd side & exploded but no damage was done. GPMG & LMG were used against the planes & the SAS Signallers used SLRs, 1 being hit in the hand by a small piece of shrapnel, he took the embedded piece out, stuck something over the cut, put the piece in his pocket & carried on firing. There were 9 planes out of 15 downed, 3 being claimed by CAP, 3 by Rapier, 2 by Galahad & 1 by us. The scene after it had quietened down was like something from a film, with the air heavy with smoke & the smell of cordite & jets disappearing over the hills trailing black smoke & then seeing black clouds as they crashed & exploded.

The 3 casualties - Seamen Macleod, Gray & Taylor are all fine, a little shaken maybe, but Macleod will probably be sent home. 4 men from EOD were killed by 20 mm fire as they were going to Galahad in a rigid raider. Everything is quiet now & we are all relaxing & getting over the shock of staring death in the face. At the moment 23:55 HMS Argonaut is being abandoned whilst they diffuse one of her unexploded bombs. Mail went off today. Argonaut ships CO. stayed on whilst bomb was diffused.

My entry for that day is pretty graphic as was the buzz, and for the young Steward, Mark Stephens, who died, it was a horrible and pointless death. The poor lad was inside the ship at his action station and, being a Steward, his role at this stage was probably first aider or fire party;

apart from his part 1 training at Raleigh he had probably never fired a weapon.

I came on watch to see the Antelope, still burning. Thick black smoke was spewing out of the centre of the ship. I stood on the Port Bridge wing. I had a Kodak 110 camera which Tania had given me as an 18th birthday present. I was watching the Antelope as the Captain was giving his daily brief. He was explaining to the rest of the ship's company about her still burning and, as he was saying this, her back broke and she snapped in two, the stern and fo'csle sticking out of the water. Her stern went down first, and the fo'csle stayed a little longer, pointing to the skies. Her 45 gun at a 45° angle in defiance, as if ready to take on the next attack. The thick black smoke soon turned to white steam as she sunk slowly beneath the waves.

I was clicking away with my camera; there were others on the bridge wing watching the death throes of this proud and brave little frigate. Little in size, but not little in crew or bravery. I heard a sound to my right, and I glanced over. Standing next two me were a couple of survivors, officers, watching as their ship, their office, their home and everything they had slipping away. One of them had tears streaming down his face, as he watched his beloved ship die. They had nothing, but the clothes on their back. Everything else was sinking under the waves. I saw the pain and the agony in that man's face and I suddenly felt very guilty, and physically sick, that I was photographing the loss of this person's home. I quickly put the camera away and moved slowly, walking backwards, to allow these men their moment of pain and grief.

She stayed with her gun pointing skyward for some time,

and was still like that during the first attack. Whether the Argentinians noticed her or not, I'll never know. I saw her gun pointing to the sky as an act of defiance, but it was never going to do anything, but increase the resolve of all that saw it as sticking two fingers up at the enemy. I'm sure if the enemy had caught sight of her, it probably gave them a morale boost to know that their attacks were hitting home.

This day was the closest I had come to being injured or killed. Friends around me dropped like flies as they were injured by shrapnel or cannon fire. The Starboard wing where I hung out for Action Stations was strafed quite badly. The 10" signal lantern which, only the day before, we had been directed to flash up and aim at the aircraft in an attempt to dazzle the pilots was shattered (later given a burial at sea).

The Captain's cabin was hit just below the bridge, bits flew around the GDP, the man next to the Captain received a glancing wound and a chunk was knocked out of the brass ring of the GDP compass repeater; and a large hole appeared in the bulkhead of the 20" signal lantern stanchion. When we saw it, it was around chest height and any one of us could have taken that 20mm cannon shell. It really made the blood run cold!

The change of tactics from the valley side of San Carlos really took us by surprise. We had the heads up by the intercepted signals, and knowing we were the main target was terrifying. I was on a much-heightened state of alertness than I had ever been. Seeing the damage to the ships around us, and ourselves, put this war into a whole new dimension. I felt, after seeing the alloys of the Antelope burn through, that an old steel ship like ours was the safest option, and we would survive a substantial attack.

What I could not have anticipated that day was that 5 of my friends were going to be injured, one seriously, and, if I had not been walking around the upper deck looking out for aircraft, it could have been me.

It was beyond horrific to see Mac on the deck, being treated by the medics, seeing the mess that was his leg splattered around the Port Bridge wing, the crimson red of his blood pooling across a large area of the deck, the white sinews of his muscles and pink flesh, sprinkled amongst the blood, standing out almost glowing white in that mass of red, and the first aid team working on him to stabilise him and save his life. His helmet had been split, his skull penetrated. There was no fire, but there was plenty of pain and I could smell the metallic tang of blood. It was strong and stuck in my nostrils, as I watched, mesmerised by the scene of my wounded friend on the deck. We knew he was still alive, but also knew he was in a really bad way. It wasn't right that we were standing around watching; we couldn't do anything because the right people were dealing with him, but I couldn't take my eyes off the vision of hell in front of me.

There was a crowd gathered around and the Skipper made a pipe on the gun crew voice circuit calmly, with authority whilst showing concern, asking the crew to give the first aid team room to work on him and for the rest of us to keep a look out for aircraft, as well as leaning over the side of the GDP to tell us all the same message. The Captain later revealed that he was warned by an old WWII hand that when people started being hit there was a temptation to turn away from weapons and attend the wounded; this could be very dangerous, and it was vital to ensure this did not happen whilst calling in the First Aid to lead in taking immediate care. Mac could have been me, he could have been anyone of us, but Mac took the hits.

I knew Mac from my days in Chatham, we joined up round about the same time in June 1980 (as did most of the youngsters on board), and we got on well. Mac was a keen photographer and I always fancied myself as bit of a potential model. He did a session for me in Chatham, with me dressed all in black, black Drainpipes and Buckskin shoes, doing my best Elvis impression at 17!

Once Mac was stabilised he was flown off to the make shift hospital known as the Red & Green Life Machine ashore at Ajax Bay that had been set up in an old sheep factory, so named because Royal Marines (with their coveted green beret) worked alongside Paras (with their maroon or red beret) to treat the injured and save lives. I was detailed off to hose down the Port Bridge wing. I was the youngest of the watch and got most of the menial tasks. Me and Bill Byrne attached the fire hose to the hydrant and got to work. I sprayed the deck, rather than sweep it. I sprayed the sinew, the flesh, the metallic blood, towards the culverts that took the water away from the decks in rough seas. We cleared away all evidence of the tragedy that had just struck us. It was an unreal scenario. I was doing it, and feeling sick doing it, but I knew that it had to be cleared so we could get ready for the next attack, and the guys on the guns could get on with what they had to do and not have any visual reminders of what had just happened to one of their crew.

I hate that image that is stuck in my head. I hate the

FEARLESS - The Diary of an 18 Year Old at War in the Falklands

vision of the bright white lines, the pink bits that were showing clearly in the pool of blood. I hate the blood. Its awful metallic smell that was stuck in my nostrils. It was awful to wash it over the side so that we could just carry on. Mac had been hit by two 20 mil cannon shells, he had a serious head injury, he had a serious leg injury and we had no knowledge of how he was doing. This was minor compared to what the Pongos and Royals ashore were having to deal with or were about to deal with, or what the Sheffield, the Ardent, Plymouth and Antelope had coped with but, for me, it was the first experience I had of casualties of war close up. One of my mates was at death's door; and if it was clear to me how easily I could have been in the same situation or even not around to be able to write this.

After the war, I first saw Mac in February 1983. I was going into a store in Portsmouth with Jackie. We walked to the main door just as Mac was heading for it. He was on a stick, and it was the first time I had seen him since he had been casevaced off the ship. I was over the moon to see him, and greeted him accordingly. We spent a couple of minutes chatting; I introduced him to Jackie, and asked how he was. He seemed in good spirits and had accepted that he was going to be medically retired with a substantial pay-out. He was going to open up a photographic studio in Chatham. I was chuffed to bits for him, because I knew he enjoyed photography from our days in Chatham and we spoke about that as well, though he admitted he'd lost those prints of me posing in the mess back then!

He appeared to have accepted that he was no longer going to serve in the Royal Navy, and he had his future planned with his compensation and pension. At 19, he was going to live on a pension! I felt for him, wondering

145

how long such a lump sum would last and whether the photography studio would support him, and how long he could live on a disability pension and be comfortable. He was a good-looking lad that had the world at his feet and it was torn away from him in an instant; now walking with a stick, and had problems with his head and memory. No matter how he tried to gloss it over that day; I felt sick to my stomach for him and I remember talking to Jackie about how sorry I was for Mac.

After this occasion, it was another 20 years before I saw Mac again. Some of the Fearless crew had started getting together for Remembrance Sunday at the Cenotaph. We could only attend if we applied for tickets through the South Atlantic Medal Association (SAMA82). I had marched a couple of times from the 15th Anniversary onwards and we kept together as a 'contingent' on the day, and in contact through the year. It was during one of these parades that I met Mac again.

Prior to his arrival, one of the lads explained how he had 'found' Mac. Barry 'Baz' Broome ex Leading Seaman and one of the San Carlos Sea Cat aimers on the GDP, had a picture framing business in Kent. One day a woman walked in with a medal in a white box. It hadn't been made up (this was how we were presented with our Falklands Medal). He commented, "A Falklands Medal. I've got one of these, how did you get this?" She explained she had been clearing her loft out and found it amongst some of her husband's things. He hadn't told her he had been to war, previously. He had told her the injuries he had were from a motor cycle accident and she went on to explain what the injuries were.

Baz checked for a name around the edge of the Medal and

instantly recognised Macleod and the Name HMS Fearless. "Bloody Hell! I know Mac! I was his 'Killick of the mess'. I've never forgotten what happened to him and have always wondered what he was doing and how he was." It transpired from Mac's wife that he hadn't been well, he struggled with many things, had very dark days and kept losing jobs.

'Baz' gave her his number with the offer for Mac to get in contact when he was ready. Eventually he did and, with help from Baz, was able to open up and talk about what had happened. Other help was provided, and Baz also put Mac in contact with an Ex-Merchant Officer who had also served down South. He gave Mac a job and understood what Mac needed when he was in his 'dark times'; as far as I am aware, Mac continued working with him.

When we met up that day, Mac explained a lot to me about his injuries and how he had hidden it all away from everybody and the problems he had faced. This was the first time he had paraded, or met, with a group of shipmates and he was very nervous, but he got on with it and it was a great day. 'Baz' did wonders helping Mac out but he just saw it as something he would do for any mate. The chance encounter with the Medal really helped one of our own.

Having taken the mick out of the gunners on the way down, and messed around/practised supporting the gun team during the quiet hours, I was then needed when the lads on the Starboard gun got shot up. There were no spare numbers on board, and the gun crew basically told me to get hold of clips of shells and pass them up.

Air Red came again, and again the silence, the waiting,

the anticipation, but this time I was wide out in the open, standing behind a 40/60 Bofor, where, less than an hour ago, 4 of my mates had been injured. The Yeoman looked out of the bridge window and saw me standing there with clip in hand. I could see by the look on his face he wasn't happy. He mouthed "What the hell are you doing? Get off there and look out." I shook my head at him, not in defiance, but because I knew they needed the extra support. He came to the bridge door and told me again. Again, I said no. I explained they had no one else, it will only be for this one attack. He shut the door and went back into the bridge. We waited anxiously, as the raid built up, it seemed like an age. Standing, scanning the horizon, praying in my mind that it wasn't going to happen. It didn't! We were all stood down and that was it for the day. I was relieved that we didn't take any more that day. It had been too close for comfort and I was on edge, more so than I had ever been.

The Captain gave his usual periodic long daily briefing across the ships tannoy, with periodic updates, and let us know that Mac was being treated and well looked after, things looked positive for him.

The regular updates over the ships tannoy from the Captain and Navigator helped those below decks understand what was happening. John Prime, kept the ships company informed from the bridge on incoming air attacks and often gave a running commentary of each wave of attacks. The first day was fairly sparse with announcements as he was to discover when he returned below decks for the first time in forty eight hours on the 21st May-

'That evening on 21 May (D Day), having been already awake and on Bridge duty for 43 hours, I was at last was able to go below to the Wardroom and get something to eat. Perhaps too casually I said to the PO Chef behind the counter that "that was a hell of day, wasn't it". What I received back was as forthright as it was unexpected – words to the effect that it was all right for you lot on the upper decks, but it was horrendous for us below. Just getting Air raid warning red followed by Take Cover, Take Cover, Take Cover and sometimes Brace, Brace, Brace did not really inform, just made people scared. I replied, perhaps worn out and tired, "well what do want a sports broadcast!?" The reply was clear "Anything is better than what we received today". So I approached his captain and asked if it would be alright if I gave out more information and so it started. To begin with factual and serious, aircraft detected at x miles, aircraft inbound, aircraft sighted, etc. However, this too became repetitious, so I started to embellish with such things as "The management apologises for the late arrival of flight 123 from Buenos Aires, but assures you that it will be here shortly to bomb the s**t out of us". This was supplemented by giving out sports news items such as the Soccer and Cricket Scores. Some may remember that Sat 22 May Cup Final between Spurs and QPR went to a replay and Spurs' Argentinian Ricky Villa opted not to play. It was a draw 1 – 1. The replay was Thursday 27th and it went something like this: "Here is result of Cup Final Replay. Oh hang on there is an air raid developing. Anyway the result was 1 – 0. Yes the aircraft are definitely heading into San Carlos. Oh it was to Spurs; Glen Hoddle penalty in 6th minute. Take Cover, Take Cover, Take Cover. Aircraft coming down starboard side. Bombs in water, no explosions." Lt Cdr John Prime.'

These broadcasts did a lot to help the morale of all the troops and ship's company onboard. They were also another example of excellent leadership in listening, taking onboard and actioning what the 'staff' say.

Ready for action!

20mm bullet hole

Walkabout Management - Capt with RM Sgt Ian Woolhead

Captured weapon put to good use

Exeter Sea Dart
Courtesy Gary 'Brigham' Young HMS Penelope

Fearless & Norland

Fearless and Exeter Dave Dolan
Courtesy Dave Dolan

Fearless Under Attack

Galahad

Harrier Emergengy refuelling stop

HMS Antelope Final Moments - Kevin's own

HMS Plymouth burns

Me in action Flashing

Miss Fearless Takes a Ride

Ron & Skipper

Pass Out Parade 16 and a Deputy Class Leader

21

Argentine National Day Disaster

Tue 25th

A fairly quiet day. Only attacked once by 2 fighter Skyhawks A4 bombers @ about 15:30. We had our heads down (in the v/s store), & were woken suddenly by the sound of machine gun fire, and just as we were stepping outside there was a huge explosion as a 500 lb exploded very close to our Port bow, causing the ship to shudder, from the blast. Had word that a big raid was building in the N.W. We were all prepared & waiting, there was a deadly silence over the whole ship (which now comes every time Air Raid Warning Red is sounded) but it never came. Instead they concentrated on Coventry & Broadsword. 16 planes attacked them & their main target appeared to be Coventry, she was hit mid-ships by two 500lb bombs which exploded straight away causing severe damage & in just over half an hour she was keeling over & had to be abandoned. Again helos were on the scene in minutes & the Broadsword, which was also hit, but the bomb went straight through causing flooding aft from a broken fire main was there picking up survivors. I heard the news that she was sinking at 19:10, but there was no news of 'Faz'. By 20:00 she had keeled over completely hull side up. 100 survivors had been picked up by Broadsword & several by helos. About 21:30 we heard that the Atlantic Conveyor had been hit by 2 Exocet fired from 2 Super Entendards, obviously meant for Invincible, but she fired CHAFF confusing the missiles homing system, throwing them off course & unfortunately they were directed then to Ant Co. One Chinook was saved the rest were destroyed.

The 2 a/c that attacked us didn't hit any targets & were destroyed - 1 by Rapier right over our heads exploding & sending bits everywhere. Again the guns crew copped it, but only 1 bloke, who was sent sprawling across the deck as he was hit by the jets canopy; he wasn't hurt & he got up straight away to claim his piece. The BBC crew were on board to film the day's events but they missed that piece of action and there was no more.

Twelve jets were splashed yesterday on the first raid, there were 5 jets but Coventry splashed 2 with her Sea Dart, CAP got 1 Rapier 1 & Plymouths Sea Cat got 1. On the Coventry attack 7 were splashed by CAP & Broadsword combined.

We got ourselves a POW who ejected when he got hit, he had his leg smashed so was sent ashore.
Had a RAS.

This was probably the worst day of the war for me. We always knew that the 25th May (25 de Mayo) was going to be tough. It is the Argentine National Day, and intel indicated that they would throw everything at us. In the few short days that we had been at war properly, we had pretty much destroyed their Air Force. The pilots were brave, amazing fliers, but they could not escape the barrage of fire that met them as they came down 'Bomb

Alley', the Sea Wolf and Sea Dart missile systems that were effective in the right theatre and the Harriers that waited for them as they tried to scurry home.

We had one small attack and it scared me rigid, as I wasn't expecting it. Pleasingly, the aircraft that attacked, and narrowly missed us never made it back home. Two less to worry about for the future! We were already all talking about the demise of the Argentine Air Force, thinking they couldn't have many aircraft left to attack us with and were feeling a little relieved, though not totally relaxed.

As we had been getting very little sleep over the past few days, the Senior Rates of the Department had allowed those that were not officially on watch to grab a break in between attacks and only if the intel indicated a break. We were fortunate to have the store on the upper deck and the flags to make a comfortable mattress and blankets. We wrapped ourselves in Ensigns and Union Flags to keep warm but, if the need arose, we were already prepared to meet Davy Jones, if our number was up! We had just settled down, to grab some kip, when the guns opened fire unexpectedly. We were all up and out in seconds as the attack took place and, as we stepped onto the Port signal deck, we caught the loud explosion and massive plume of water that was thrown up from the blast. It was very close and probably the closest we had been to being hit by bombs. Apart from the shock and the noise, there was no damage to the ship or the crew (though rumour has it that a 'Royal' was getting his head down in 2C mess and was thrown out of his pit, breaking his arm).

That was our action for the day. My starting entry appears very non-plussed and I think, at the time, we just accepted that we would be attacked at some point through the day as if it was as normal as scoring on a Friday night.

Meanwhile, we got word through that a massive raid was building from the West, and all the ships in San Carlos were called to Action Stations. The place was silent, referring to the whole scene in San Carlos. It was a very strange sensation, to see all those ships around you and not hear a sound. All the upper deck crews were focussed on Fanning Head, the entrance to San Carlos, watching, listening, watching, and waiting for the first aircraft to appear. They never did on that day, instead, they concentrated their attack on HMS Broadsword and HMS Coventry who were outside of Falkland Sound, playing 'goalkeeper' to attack the aircraft before they got to us. Coventry used her Sea Dart Surface to Air Missile system to great effect, taking out several aircraft that day and I think, in the short time she was with us, claimed the most kills for the war. Sea Dart was a long-range weapon system and could take out aircraft over thirty miles away. They had to operate in the open for the system to be effective.

The whole attack was concentrated on those two ships who were working together to protect the amphibious operations. Broadsword took out a couple of aircraft with her Sea Wolf close in weapons system (CIWS), but during the final attack, the two ships crossed each other's paths, and the Sea Wolf became confused and locked down. Coventry, then took several bombs in the lower decks of the ship, which caused extensive damage and flooding, and within twenty minutes, the whole ship had keeled over.

My cousin Chief Petty Officer (CPO) Alan Fazackerly was on board Coventry. He was very close to our immediate family. He lived with Mum, his parents and my grandparents in Woolwich as a child, and they became very close. He is a few years younger than her but became like a brother to her and my Dad also. He is a great character and loved by everyone he meets. It is very difficult not to like Faz. Not knowing what had happened to him created a very anxious time for me.

I was standing on the Starboard wing, waiting for the aircraft to arrive. We heard they had attacked the 'goalkeepers', but nothing more. The Starboard bridge wing door opened and the Yeoman, George Moutter came bounding towards me. He came close, too close for what is normal distance. He spoke to me quietly, "Kevin. They've got the Coventry."

"What?"

"The Coventry, they focussed their attacks on her. She's sinking." I stared at him absorbing his words. "I know your cousin is on there, Kevin." He was calling me by my first name. There was something wrong.

"When? How long ago?" I wasn't sure what to ask or say.

"I don't know. I only know they have directed their attack at her and she is sinking. I know your cousin is on there and you needed to know. My best mate is the RS on there, and I don't know where he is. He was the best man at my wedding."

I was in a state of shock. We couldn't lose Faz. He was our favourite cousin. My parents loved him. He taught me gimbals, which we were learning in physics at school, when the HMS Torquay was in Liverpool in the late 1970s and we visited him. It was the first time I had been on a warship, and it was fantastic; we still have two 4.5 shells from the Torquay in my Mum's house. I had to clean them every week for pocket money; 'where there's muck there's brass' and they were definitely brass.

Faz also got me trooped (disciplined) for the first time in the Navy. He was OOW on HMS Victory and my brother, Paul, and I were in the Portsmouth area together. I was in training at HMS Mercury and Paul was at HMS Vernon. A call round was called and we assembled on the gangway of HMS Victory. This was a big thing for me. I was shy and in awe of Faz and Polly and only 17. We were both given the unofficial tour of the Royal Navy's flagship; then back to the Chief's mess for scran and refreshments. Several pints of CSB later, and the time for the last train to get me back on board for midnight (Cinderella leave), Faz got the Pussers out - a large tot was had! In those days, you had to show your ID card as you were leaving a Royal Naval Establishment or Dockyard. I managed to get the train to Petersfield and the 'Pusser's Tilley' back to Mercury. Reaching into my back pocket to get my ID card out at the gate, I began to panic - it wasn't there! Checking all my other pockets, looking frantic as the guard stood there with a smug smile on his face, knowing I was on my way to getting trooped.

PO of the Guard came out "Official Number?" he barked.

"D184796P PO" I responded immediately.

"Backwards!"

"P697481D." This was a test to see if I was sober or not.

"On your way JRO Porter. A report will be going to the Kelly Squadron CO and I expect you will be getting your cap!" I was seriously worried as I wandered up the Crescent Road to my block. Lo and behold, I had to 'get my cap' for Commanders table. Trembling outside in the corridor waiting for my name to be called.

"JRO Porter!" shouted the Joss.

"Sir!" as I snapped to attention.

"Quick March! (For about 10 paces) Halt! Off Cap!"

I received the lecture from the Commander about security and how a lost ID card could come into the wrong hands etc. I apologised profusely, trying to minimise the punishment.

"1 day's finable rate of pay." he announced. I was elated that I still had my shore leave.

"Are you playing hockey for Mercury today, Porter?" he asked.

"Yes Sir!" I replied proudly.

"Good. When I have finished here, I will be joining the game and taking your shirt. Dismissed."

"On Caps! Salute! About turn, quick march!"

I marched out of his office, not sure whether I was more disappointed with the loss of pay or the loss of the shirt. He did turn up, called me over and I had to take my shirt off and give it to him, for him to play. I got fifteen minutes of that game and £3.25 deducted from my pay. Faz and Polly found it hilarious when I told them what had happened.

Fortunately, Faz was rescued after an amazing act of bravery and being the last person to leave the Coventry as she was on her side. He had gone back inside her four times to search for survivors and this was no surprise to me and the measure of the man I knew and loved.

I've learned that the Commodore personally despatched every possible helicopter immediately he heard of the strike on Coventry. Thanks to him and the marevellous aircrew, Faz was picked up by a helo, which landed on our deck for refuelling. He asked for a pen and paper and he wrote me a message letting me know he was safe. He handed it to one of the WAFUs to get it to RO Porter on the Bridge. He'd folded the paper and written my name on the outside. Unfortunately, it never got to me, which was difficult for me but also created unnecessary confusion and despair for his family. Mai, his wife, was told he was missing presumed dead, then they had found him, then missing presumed dead – it went on for a while like this and must have been awful for her and the 3 children. If I had received the note, I'm sure I would have been allowed to send a telegram home and a signal to the Invincible on which his brother Dave was serving also.

I also saw a completely different side to Yeoman Moutter that day and from that day onwards. He had looked worried and shocked when he was talking to me, and in the coming days we shared a common bond of waiting for news of those we cared about. He continually checked up on me whilst we were waiting for the casualty signal to come through. He had been tough on us youngsters since we joined the ship, and especially so during our way down. It was all for a good reason, and it worked for us all. I really did get to like him.

The other big shock that day was the STUFT ship Atlantic Conveyor. She was carrying extra aircraft, Harriers, and helicopters, including Chinooks, for transporting the troops across the islands and laden with stores of all sorts – tents, spare parts, weapons, ammunition. She was an important part of the Task Force and was making her way to unload on the islands. Two Super Ententard aircraft carrying the French built Exocet missile, flying very low over the water, attacked the Task Force. The missiles were devastating. They had never been used in anger prior to the Falklands War and the sinking of HMS Sheffield and so this was a perfect testing ground for them. Initially built for ship-to-ship attacks, the French had adapted them to be fitted to aircraft and it was widely felt (though may not be proven) that some French engineers had stayed behind in Argentina to continue to oversee the fittings and ensure they worked.

For years, I despised the French nation for this. Only later did I find out that the French President, Mitterrand, supported Mrs Thatcher and MI6 in preventing the selling of any more missiles to Argentina; they had a very limited stock, our intel indicating probably no more than 8. They'd already fired four, so we were hoping that would be it. Unfortunately, the pilots picked up some large targets and released the missile from some thirty six miles out; the missile skims about 10 ft. above the surface of the water and its built-in radar constantly searches for the nearest and largest target.

Once a missile is detected by ships, they have all sorts of methods of deflecting an attack. This can include electronic measurements, firing rockets full of aluminium foil that, when released, create a large signature for the radar to pick up, and also using helicopters as decoys. The counter measures worked for the Invincible, but unfortunately Atlantic Conveyor did not have any of these countermeasures fitted, and the missile radars though confused, picked up on another target and sadly went straight for her, with devastating effect.

The final part of my diary entry that day was the mention of our first POW, a pilot that had ejected after being hit. It was clear that the Argentine authorities, as well as other atrocities we had heard about, also had no scruples about the use of their propaganda machine with their own military. The pilot that was bought on board was convinced he was on a ghost ship, as his squadron had been told that there were very few ships left in San Carlos and HMS Fearless had been sunk. They must have felt totally unprepared for the truth when they reached San Carlos and he had difficulty believing he was still alive and had not ended up in hell when he was brought on board. Whether it was the pain, the morphine or the shock, he took a lot of convincing that he was still alive, being looked after on board HMS Fearless by the British Royal Navy. Eventually he was shipped off to the Red & Green Life Machine to be operated on. It struck me as very odd that an air force pilot of such intelligence and skill would rather believe he had died and gone to hell than that he had been duped by his superiors with a made-up story about the destruction of warships.

22

Sneakies

Wed 26th

Yet again a quiet day without being attacked, but Air Raid Warning Red sounded, massive raid building up. No planes came but disappeared around Port Stanley area, obviously the airfield's in use again. Did an SBS landing very early in the morning (03:00) under total darkness & silence. We went within 1/2 a mile of shore & it was all done smoothly & within an hour. When completed we made our way back to the anchorage. Been told to put in request form for RO1s. End of day & still no news of 'Faz', God knows how they're feeling at home, but I'm cracking up here.

We or the Intrepid would often sneak out under cover of darkness to do troop insertions. Usually, Special Forces. It was a risky strategy to have such large capital ships sailing around the Islands at night and, even though we knew we were safe from air attack, everybody was on edge during these operations.

It is a bit of a misnomer to say that we 'sneaked' anywhere or that the missions were silent. The communications and people may have been, but the noise from the ship's funnels was enough to wake the dead down there. The air was so clear, that sound carried for miles. As the war went on, we could hear the Royal Artillery shelling enemy positions near to Stanley some 60 miles away. What was true though was the totality of the darkness. When there was no moon you could barely see your hands in front of your face. We had a very shallow draft, and I have even experienced the ship being 'beached' whilst on exercise in Norway, so we were ideal for these sorts of insertions. We were faster than the LSLs (not much though) and definitely quicker than our LCUs.

The Chief Yeoman (CCY), Mick Tapping, told me I was ready to go up to the next rate. This meant I had completed my Task Book to move me forward and, being 18, I was old enough now to become a real Radio Operator 1st Class. It meant I would have a star on my badge like the rest of the Tactical Team and a wage increase. It didn't stop them all from treating me as their 'sprog', I was still the youngest and least experienced. The CCY gave me a pep talk and told me that I was good enough to be a Chief Yeoman by the time I was 27. He claimed that he had been the youngest CCY in the fleet at 28, and I could beat that record. I had the intelligence and attitude to go all the way he said. I was proud and pleased by this, though, I never achieved it for reasons that will become clear later.

We still had no news on the survivors from the Coventry. You may think that, with all our modern technology, information would have come through quickly but the Coventry had lost a number of men, and the survivors were scattered around the various ships and the hospital at Ajax Bay. In my role I knew how difficult it would be to gather the correct information but I was struggling not knowing where Faz was, or if he was even alive. I was constantly imagining him being blown to pieces by the bombs, or drowned out there in the icy waters of the South Atlantic. It didn't bear thinking about, but I just couldn't help it. It was on my mind all the time, and I got so little sleep during the period.

23

Splashed

Thurs 27th

"Faz' wasn't on the missing list or injured personnel so must be safe, but don't know where. Found out at 03:00 just before I went on watch. Put in request for RO1s. Quiet day until about 19:40 when four Mirages attacked shore HQ & an ammo dump & a hospital on the other side of the water causing several explosions & fires but not hitting the main dump. 3 blokes killed one of which died on here & 20 odd injured. Left 'Bomb Alley' to rendezvous with Antrim & collect Major General Moore RM CLFFI (Commander Land Forces Falkland Islands). 2 of the planes being shot down both being hit by our Port 40/60 but Rapier claimed one.

I went up to do my watch early, as I couldn't sleep. I got called into the office by the Yeoman who had a clipboard full of signals in his hand. He handed me the board and asked "Is Faz on there?" The top signal was the casualty list for HMS Coventry. I scanned through the names of the casualties and those souls that couldn't be found. I almost cheered with relief that I couldn't find his name but it made for sombre reading. I didn't know any of the names on the list but, even so, all the names on there were either dead or injured, some very seriously. However, a massive weight was lifted. I couldn't send anything home as, I was told, the MOD were dealing with this, and if there was a mistake, then it could be painful for the family. Little did we know the true story that was unfolding with the confusion back home! Thankfully though, Mai did receive final confirmation that he was alive.

The Argentine Air Force had obviously had a battering. The day was very quiet, though we were no less alert. Suddenly four aircraft appeared, screaming down the valley, and split into two formations. One couple went to the North side of San Carlos and the other south. On the southern side, was our 'Red & Green Life Machine' field hospital.

The aircraft were flying low level, we couldn't do much about those on the Starboard side, so most of us were over on the Port side spotting the aircraft. The young aimer on the 40/60, Alan Moody, had started to engage the aircraft. I had them in my binoculars and watched helplessly as they dropped their bombs on the hospital. I also saw the 40/60 shells tracking ahead of the aircraft. Alan had tracked them in and had his gun aimed at their height. He was firing ahead of them, and I watched amazed as I saw two shells smack into the main frame of the first aircraft, it shuddered slightly and carried on, then I watched two more puffs in the 'second aircraft. Others on the Port side had seen this and we were all cheering. We watched the aircraft disappear over the hills, smoke pouring from them. They were not going to make it home. The pilots ejected over West Falklands and were picked up by their own men. We all gathered around the gun; Alan had the biggest grin ever on his face! It was an amazing piece of gunnery; a Second World War gun taking out two modern jet fighters. He had really thought about what he was doing when he attacked these aircraft, and it worked with great effect.

Sadly though, the hospital was hit and two men were killed and several injured. The other death was a Royal Marine at the HQ on the other side. The hospital also had two unexploded bombs stuck in the roof and metal rafters. It is now legendary, and well known, that the surgery never ever stopped whilst the bombs were there. Lives continued to need saving and the brave actions of the surgeons and medical teams also had the added impact of boosting morale, as others in the hospital heard about this show of defiance to the enemy and the commitment to the injured. It didn't matter who you were once you were injured, the medical team treated each man the same way and with the same respect and dignity.

We had placed an ammunitions dump next door to the hospital. In theory this should have been a tactical cock-up on our part, if the enemy had been taking any notice of the Geneva Convention, perhaps we would have been reprimanded for it. As it was, not only had the bombs hit the hospital, but one landed smack bang in the middle of the ammunition. How so few people were injured and killed during that attack is nothing short of a miracle. There were shells and bullets firing everywhere. As with the Antelope, we watched the ammo explode through the night. It was a sight to see but we were not enjoying a fireworks display; those in the hospital were at risk and we needed this ammunition. We were a long way from home, and it was not going to be easily replaced.

We had bit of a break after this day. Under the cover of darkness, we set sail for South Georgia. We were to rendezvous with one of the STUFT ships, the QEII, which had 5 Brigade embarked and the Senior Army Officer who was to take responsibility for the remainder of the war. This was normal practice, and in no way reflected the ability of the officers of the Amphibious Command. The amphibious phase was over, and the command needed to be handed over to someone more senior and with different tactical experience to manage the land war.

It was a relief to be sailing away from the Islands, but I could not fully relax. As tired as I was after the past 8 days, it was still difficult to sleep soundly and not worry about what may be out there. We were fairly confident once we got further East of the Islands as we knew we were out of range of any air attacks. We knew their navy had stayed in port afraid of straying too far for fear of attack by submarines after the sinking of the Belgrano. This was a huge advantage to the Task Force, no matter how controversial the sinking of the Belgrano by the nuclear submarine HMS Conqueror was it prevented a lot more bloodshed and death. It also proved that the Argentinian armed forces were not working together as a team and this really boosted our morale. I knew we would go back though; it was only a temporary respite.

24

Goose Green

Fri 28th
At sea. Left the TEZ. Darwin taken by Paras. Only 20 Paras killed & 250 Argies killed.

Sat 29th
Goose Green taken & a total of 1200 or more prisoners taken, even more after they tried to recapture it. Still at sea.

These were the first land battles to take place. There was a lot of pressure from the powers that be back in the UK for the Task Force to demonstrate our strength and resolve, and also for the country and the world to recognise that even with the amount of losses we had suffered with the warships, we were still capable of winning these Islands back.

The Amphibious Command were not happy about moving forward so quickly, and initially had planned to send a recce platoon out to Goose Green to get the 'lay of the land' prior to a full-on assault. This was over-ruled by London and therefore Brigadier Julian Thomson Royal Marines had to re-order his battle plans.

2 Para took on a force 4 times larger, and still managed to defeat the Argentinians. It wasn't an easy defeat by any means, many good men were killed during the battle and, sadly, afterwards. News soon got to us, during the battle, that the Colonel of 2 Para, H. Jones, had been killed whilst attacking a machine gun post.

We got the signal 'Sunray Down' over the Command net. It was a shock to hear those words for real. The first time I had heard it was on exercise in Norway a few months before. It was acceptable then, we knew it was only for exercise, but this time, it was "Shit, what next?" Even then I questioned, as many of us did, why a Colonel was so far up front and not conducting the battle from HQ. It was his decision and apparently how he led his troops. It cost him his life. His 2nd IC, Major Keeble, took command and rallied his troops.

They were not all conscripts as the media and intel had us believe. They were very professional soldiers who fought hard, and with passion for a land they believed in. We had a very disciplined, fit and determined army that wanted revenge for all they had seen and experienced whilst sitting on the hillsides surrounding Bomb Alley. They also had the history and honour of the Parachute Regiment to uphold. They were first into battle with the Royal Marines and Welsh & Scots Guards infantry regiments taking up the rear. There was a lot at stake for the regiment, the Task Force and Great Britain. If they failed, then we would all fail. As Mrs Thatcher famously said, "Failure – the possibilities do not exist." These Paras were fired up and were not going to let go.

Major Keeble eventually called the Argentine bluff. He realised we were running low on ammunition and the troops were shattered, so he boldly gave the Argentines an ultimatum.

"Surrender, to avoid any more bloodshed. We are a more superior force and we will bring all our power down on you."

This was accepted, and one thousand two hundred Argentinian Soldiers, Airmen and Sailors marched out behind a military band to lay down their arms. We had just four hundred and fifty Paras. I almost called them men, but with what they did during that battle, it would almost be an insult to their courage, strength and skill, they were practically super human!

25

Exocet – What Exocet?

Sun 30th
*Still at sea but on our way back to Bomb Alley. Had an
Entendard threat, but nothing happened.*

The weariness was setting in and a fair bit of trepidation
about going back into the hell of Bomb Alley. The word
'but' has so many meanings, and I remember the feeling
as I wrote this short entry. I was scared. We had escaped
thus far, but how long was our luck going to hold out?
We were a bloody big ship sitting in a very small valley,
surely something was going to happen to us? There was
nothing for it though, I just had to get on with it and accept
our fate.

We had picked up 5 Brigade right down in South Georgia.
I'd heard various pipes about the scenery as we were
travelling further south. I remember being disturbed by
a pipe about a large iceberg being close by. I lifted my
head off the pillow, and it dropped straight back down
again. I just couldn't be bothered to go up top and have
a look. I think tiredness had finally set in. There are very
few people that have the opportunities that we had in the
Royal Navy, at that time, to see some of the most stunning

sights in nature; I didn't take it for granted but I really was just too tired to move so I let this one slide silently by.

The joy of being a 'Bunting' was that you were almost constantly connected to the Operations Room via the bridge and other voice circuits. When a threat was detected a code-word was transmitted as a Flash message. A flash (Z) overrides all security e.g. silent transit. The world would be silent and then suddenly you would hear with urgency in the voice:

> "Flash, Flash, Flash. This is call sign Flash code-word,
> I say again Flash code-word out" or written as:
> "Z de call sign, Z Code word IMI Z Code word +"

The circuit would then go silent again. As soon as Z was received, the RO would shout out Z as the signal was coming in and repeat it as it was being said. We all knew the code words for the various radars, fire control radars and missile homing radars. They were drummed into us in training, on exercise and on workup to war.

Whilst the Exocet missile had been used to devastating effect on 'The Shiny Sheff' and Atlantic Conveyor, we knew Argentina had a limited supply of these devastating missiles and we were almost certain that they had used up their quota. We were not complacent about this, but we also felt we were too far east to be affected by any attack and were out of range.

As always, we on the bridge wings and upper deck lookouts were sharp and focussed, scanning the horizon, just in case. The threat passed as quickly as the Z message that sent the warning. It was just another part of the war for me, and, for once, one that didn't hold a lot of fear.

The Exocet missile was the most feared weapon in the war for many sailors. I had a healthy respect for the threat but, because of where we were most of the time, I never worried too much about it. It had to be launched in the open and would never work inside the land mass of the Falkland Islands.

However; for Trevor Ramshaw a young RO1 (T) on board HMS Exeter stationed out with the carrier group, it was a different matter as this extract from his diary shows:

*'...Suddenly and without warning, "**CONTACT BEARING 090**" was screamed over the Ops room intercom. Within an instant it was like pandemonium in the Ops room as they scanned their radar screens, "**MULTIPLE CONTACTS BEARING 090**" was the next report I heard shouted over the intercom, four planes had been detected at about 50 miles from a bearing 090. They were two Super Entendards each with an escort. The Super Entendards were Exocet-carrying jets and we knew they still had some missiles left to fire. The Argentine Air Force had five of these aircraft, with the capability to carry and deliver Exocet missiles to their chosen targets...*

I knew we were about to be attacked, but nothing could have prepared me for what I was about to go through in the next 10 minutes...

I felt physically sick with fear and excitement, as the darts streaked towards their targets. I was scanning out of the window on the Starboard side of the bridge, but could see nothing. It seemed like ages had passed, but in reality it was only a matter of a second or two. The adrenalin was pumping hard and my heart was absolutely pounding away as I kept scanning.

Suddenly a whistle went off in the Ops room and I heard someone shout "Handbrake" over the intercom. The whistle sounded again as another missile was detected. The four contacts had suddenly become six as two Exocet missiles were released from the Super Entendards. A second later the emergency warning for enemy missile came over the radio circuit. I screamed at the OOW **"Enemy missile bearing 135 sir!"** *"Roger* **that"** *came the reply. Almost immediately came a report of another missile on a similar bearing, which I also reported to the OOW. Another* **"Roger that"** *was received.*

We were in deep shit and I really did think we had a good chance of being hit. I was scared shitless.... **"HIT THE DECK, HIT THE DECK, ITS COMING FOR US!"** *I couldn't believe what was happening, we were going to die for sure. I couldn't see a way out of this one. I threw myself on the deck underneath the comms intercom and lay next to the Chief Yeoman who had been on the bridge throughout. I thought now's the time to smack him one if you really want to. I couldn't believe I was having these thoughts. Here I was about to die and all I could think of was smacking the Chief!*
We were laid on the floor for about 20 seconds. They were the longest 20 seconds in my life. I suddenly found myself praying, saying "Please God, don't let it hit us. Please God don't let it hit us". I thought of my parents and sisters and I really didn't think I would see them again as I lay there waiting for the impact." Extracted from Planes, Bombs and Missiles, A personal account of the Falklands War. Trevor Ramshaw.

Fortunately, with great skill and courage the Exeter took

out 2 of the aircraft and 1 of the missiles with her Sea Dart missile system and, with the use of CHAFF, distracted the other missile away from the ship and it crashed into the sea.

Trevor and I joined the navy on the same day, went through basic training together and also our communication training at HMS Mercury. It is amazing the different experiences we had and the emotions we felt in the same war - 1 war 2 battles!

We sailed back into Bomb Alley under the cover of darkness and weighed anchor. We spent the next 7 days, nipping in and out at night, returning before sunrise, or keeping things maintained on the ship, and getting some sleep.

It was at this point that we realised the Argentine Air Force was now pretty much spent. We would get the odd warning of a raid building, aircraft circling far off to the East; our men on the ground in Argentina, reporting when aircraft were taking off and what direction they were heading. We also got reports from our men on the ground about mutinies that were happening at the airbases. The troops and I believe some of the officers were getting hacked off with the lies that they were being told about the aircraft returning to other bases rather than their own home bases. The Argentine home forces were starting to understand they were on a loser and they were being lied to. This gave me a great sense of relief, but not enough for us to stand down. We still had a land war to fight, and there were still Pucaras out there.

The Airport at Stanley was still in use, and supplies were being flown in daily. These planes came in generally low under the radar, unloaded whatever it was they were unloading and flew off again.

The weather was now starting to turn, and it was definitely getting colder. One morning coming up on watch, there was a covering of snow on the decks and over the hillsides; it was looking more and more like Cumbria every day.

I stopped writing in my diary because I didn't want to fill it up with nothing. It really was a quiet period that gave us a bit of breathing space. Dad had always said that active service was 5% action, 95% boredom!

26

HMS Plymouth Fire-Fighting

Tue 8th June

Sorry but nothing has happened on our part of the war until today when we got attacked by some Skyhawks & Mirages (usual routine). But none actually came near us, but they attacked Plymouth and she took three bombs plus a UXB. She had some fires on board but they were put out. Her 4.5 was damaged but they got that working late on, the PO's mess (under 4.5), galley, funnel (went straight through), & one in her mortar well. One of our LCUs was attacked by four Skyhawks, sinking her & killing 6 blokes, two survived, they didn't really stand a chance they aren't very big & they only have 1 GPMG on the back & the murdering bastards attacked her with missiles & cannon fire, it was seen by a couple of Harriers on a training flight & they attacked them getting them all, 1 crashing into the side of the hill & another hitting the sea, the others were shot down. 2 LSLs Tristram & Galahad were hit, Galahad was hit in her vehicle deck where hundreds of Welsh Guards & 29 Cdo & 42 were waiting to go ashore, killing, we think, nearly 200, I believe Derek Snelson is on there but I don't know if he was ashore. They were both abandoned, because of the size of the fires & they were full of ammunition, so there wouldn't be any more lives lost.

We had a brief quiet spell. The 8th June was memorable for many reasons. My diary was starting to appear rather blasé by my entries. Being attacked may have become usual routine, but to see a ship, steaming across the entrance to San Carlos, billowing smoke and flames was not normal! HMS Plymouth, an old Rothesay class frigate and made of steel, managed to take the hits and explosions and still float. She sailed back into San Carlos to a safe anchorage and teams of fire fighters from HMS Fearless and others were flown out to the ship to help the ship's company deal with the fires and damage.

Fire-Fighting on HMS Plymouth

This is an extract taken from MEM Colin Pearson HMS Fearless' diary of his experience fighting those fires. Colin was also at Chatham with me and we joined the ship together. He had also just turned 18 and had to do this...

This was the busiest day of my war and also the saddest. It started like any other day. Closing up at action station. Threats of Air Raids, Jets skirting the limits of our planes' capabilities, playing games and ultimately getting shot down if they played the game badly.

Around 10 o'clock a broadcast came over telling us that a large raid was building and was due in shortly. The fun and games began shortly after.

Take cover!!! Take Cover!!!

Raid coming in from the stern.

Splash one. One of the frigates had just shot a Sky

Hawk out of the sky, no survivors.

No survivors! That bang we have just heard above our heads was the end of a life. It was really strange to think about it that way. I still held no real hatred towards the Argentinians. I could not quite come to terms with the fact that we were actually killing people just because our Governments could not solve their problems through diplomatic means. It's always left to people such as myself who never really joined the Navy to be part of killing. I joined because of the depressed job prospects in the area that I lived in. What am I doing here? I have to wonder if I would have had the balls to actually shoot someone. I convinced myself that the only reason I am thinking these thoughts is because I have the luxury to do so. If I was out there faced by the enemy, and it was either him or me, I know who would be going home in a body bag. I shouldn't be thinking this shit at my age! I should be thinking about having fun and enjoying life.

Mobile Fire-fighting team to the flight deck, at the double.

HMS Plymouth has been hit in the last raid and needs assistance.

As I was part of the team I got permission to leave my fire and repair party position and begun to assemble the pre-arranged equipment down in the tank deck. It was a pain in the arse getting through the ship as it was well shut down for action. When we had assembled we were putting all our equipment into cargo netting for the chopper to pick up. I and three of the other lads were dressing in Fearnought suits as our job was to get in there and actually fight the fires.

Whilst we were waiting for the chopper to arrive I checked my equipment, we all checked each other's equipment and were ready for the 'off'. I looked around and it looked quite a strange scene. I remember it looking like an untidy bedroom. Everything has its place but nothing's in the place you expect it. Helicopters were hiding in little ravines by the shore line, landing craft were darting into the middle of an open piece of water not wanting to get too close to any "target" and a Type 42 destroyer, HMS Exeter, was violently manoeuvring, trying to get into a better position before the next raid comes in. I was much more used to seeing the navy in perfect order. Anchors dropped, sufficient space between each ship so as not to foul any swings due to a wind change and in front of my eyes seemed to be complete disarray. I liked it better when I couldn't see anything.

We could see the Plymouth coming through the entrance of San Carlos, she was a long way off but it was possible to see she was smoking heavily and blowing off steam. At least she was blowing off steam or we were about to go into a very unpleasant situation indeed.

Our helicopter arrived. Normally there was a queue of choppers waiting to land on our deck but they all moved aside so this Sea King could land. We loaded on our equipment and he took off. I nearly shit myself. This guy banked over so hard I thought I was going to fall out. In the chopper our boss went over the order of things again. My mate and I were to be team A and the other lads team B. We had no idea what the situation was, only that the crew was quickly running out of usable breathing apparatus. They still had fires on board, some flooding from cannon fire below the waterline and were beginning to list heavily to stbd. This was going to be fun! We arrived at the scene quite quickly; the Plymouth was still under way trying to get to the relative safety of San Carlos. We could see a lot of smoke billowing from what looked like a hole in the flight deck. We were later to find out that it was a fire in the aft Petty Officer's mess. Because of the smoke coming from the stern we were not aware of the damage on the stern deck. The pilot attempted to make an approach and was waved off. The aft mortar room had been hit by a 'bouncing bomb' it came in through the port side and bounced through the mortar room before ricocheting of the mortars and dropping overboard. This left live ammunition strewn around the stern area and stopped us from landing on the flight deck. The pilot moved forward to see where he could drop us off. It was obvious that they needed urgent assistance. As we moved forward we could see a large gaping hole in the funnel, this was probably the reason for the plumes of steam we seen earlier. We could see a medic attending to a patient on the Port gun deck. This was the first thought I had given to casualties. When you see a ship hit you think of it as an object which has just being damaged, it takes more thought to understand that people damage much easier than ships.

The pilot was waved to the bow of the ship. With all the antennas on the upper deck area it was the only safe place to drop us off. The pilot did a great job. He came in sideways and moved over the bow until we had a place to jump out. With all the gear we had on it was still a bit of a drop. We off-loaded our gear with the help of Plymouth's crew and made our way down the Port side. It was at this point I saw my first casualty.

The guy we seen earlier being tended to was actually an old friend of mine from my days in Chatham, Jack Warner. I stopped to talk to him but quickly realised that he had a large 'M' painted on his forehead. I knew from the training we had on the way down that he had been administered morphine. I asked the medic if he would be OK, he just shrugged his shoulders. He had been walking through a hatch when the bombs hit and it exploded in his face. He had a rather large piece of hatch sticking in his head. I also noticed at this time the crew. A lot of them were actually still in shock. They looked somehow detached, anyone not involved with the fire-fighting or damage control seemed to be just sitting around. I didn't expect this at all and was taken by surprise. It was an effect of battle never talked about. It was something which, given the intense situation we were finding ourselves in really looked out of place. This made me feel even more detached from the situation. I was in 'auto-pilot' reacting to training only and not really thinking too deeply about the actual situation. Our only objective was to put the fires out and stop the flooding.

We continued on down the Port side onto the flight deck and down onto the stern deck. We had to cross over to the stbd side as the Port ladder had been blown away. When we were on the stern deck we could see the damage left by the bouncing bomb. Crew were throwing live ammunition overboard from the damaged magazine not even thinking of the potential dangers, no one was, get on with it and do what was necessary to save the ship. This was a time when personal safety was not the main concern. This was another by-product of battle, which was not expected. It was the real part of war, which the politicians know nothing about prior to breaking off negotiations. It made people carry out extraordinary acts which they would not even dream of doing in different circumstances.

The Plymouth's Chief Stoker briefed us. He told us that they had a fire blazing in the aft PO's mess, which is where all the smoke was coming from and also a possible fire in the galley. My mate and I were to check out the fire in the galley whilst the other team was to tackle the PO's mess. The Chief looked a little worse for wear. He had obviously been inhaling smoke as he had dark trails coming from his nose and his eyes were watering heavily. Chief Stokers are desperately mindful of their ships and this guy was no exception. It looked like it would have broken his heart had the ship been lost.

We carried out final check of our equipment, our boss gave us a little word of encouragement, "Get in there and put the fucking fire out" he said laughing. It was a really good move as we were all feeling a little apprehensive about going into a burning, heavily listing ship to put out fires. If this thing continued to roll how the hell would we get out? Would we get out? His words of encouragement put us at ease a little and then the door was opened. Masses of thick acrid smoke came billowing out and it was evident that if we were not able to put out the fires the ship may be lost. We had just watched the Antelope burn over several days and break in two then sink. I didn't want the same thing to happen to the Plymouth, especially with me on it. The crew looked on as we went through the hatch with our hoses fully charged. We continued on past the PO's mess to the galley. The fire in the mess was raging and we could feel the heat through our suits. The second team began fighting that fire whilst we struggled on to the galley. It was a pain in the arse pulling those hoses. In all the exercises we'd done we always had well placed hose tenders to take some of the weight of the hoses. The smoke was so bad here that we had to drag them ourselves. We got to the galley and got into position to effect and entry. No.2 on water wall and No. 1 on Jet.

We began to advance and because of the pressure of the water coming from the hose and the greasy tiles of the galley, every time we let go of the ranges we were sliding all over the place. My mate and I were in fits of laughter, quite strange considering the circumstances. We had to tuck the hoses between our legs and pull ourselves through the galley the best we could. The smoke was really thick so we had to keep together or we would quickly lose sight of each other. We were giggling the whole way through it like school kids. As we advanced I kicked something which felt like a body. The Chief hadn't told us anyone was inside but we had to check it out. I told my mate and we aimed our hoses to shield us from any heat and we both crouched down together. What I had kicked was actually a big bag of potatoes. We were off again, laughing like idiots.

It was obvious that any fire in the galley had been extinguished so we made our way back down the passageway. The second team was still fighting the fire in the PO's mess so we assisted by boundary cooling adjoining compartments the best we could. We had put an awful lot of water in to the ship but luckily we had got a hold of any remaining fires. The PO's mess fire was extinguished and we all made our way back out to the stern. The ship was listing even more heavily now but luckily another ship had been alongside whilst we were inside and dropped off some of their breathing apparatus. The Plymouth's damage control teams were back in action and immediately set about removing the water from below decks. They got a generator running and started their pumps. Things were quickly under control and we were told we would be returning to our ship by landing craft as all the helicopters were tasked with more important operations.

We had a little time to reflect on what we had done and it seemed quite funny that we could find something amusing about being in such in a dangerous situation. I suppose it's the brain's way of convincing you that training rules when really you should be dropping everything and going home to somewhere safe.

The ship was a mess. The ammunition had all been thrown overboard but there was a real mess to clean up. The mortar room was a write-off one of the mortar tubes was all bent. The hole in the side where the bomb had entered had taken a section of a life ring with it. It now looked like a half-eaten doughnut. The funnel had a neat entry hole and a massive exit hole. It looked like it does on the comical movie portrayals. There was a small amount of smoke coming from the hole in the flight deck where the bomb had entered the PO's mess. The Plymouth's crew was watching this area in case the fire flared up again. There were bits of metal strewn all over the deck and after picking up a piece I realised it was actually shrapnel from the bombs which had hit the ship. I was amazed how sharp these edges were and could see how easy it was for someone to be killed by such a piece of metal flying at God knows what speed. I went up to see if my mate was still on board, but had been told that he had been flown off. I couldn't believe what time it was and how long we had spent on board. We had been on there for hours but it seemed as if we had just arrived.

Our lift arrived and the time was now around 4:30 in the afternoon. We loaded our equipment aboard and left the ship. The crew was still very busy and paid little attention to us leaving. I was glad to see the list was disappearing and the crew now had control of the situation. We had to pass some equipment over to the frigate which dropped it off earlier and after dropping a set of breathing apparatus overboard we were finally on our way back to our ship. The fun wasn't over however. On the way back to the ship we heard these planes come screaming in from our stern. Guns were firing in all directions and we could see missiles and tracer bullets coming from all directions. The marine on the front of the landing craft we were on begun firing his General Purpose Machine Gun (GPMG) and it was the first time I really felt exposed. One half of me said get down and the other was fascinated with what I was seeing. No quicker had the plane arrived than they were gone again.

We arrived back on board and off-loaded our equipment. We were not normally allowed to shower during daylight hours but I'm afraid we didn't take any notice during this occasion. I had actually pissed myself on a few occasions, as we were soaked to the skin anyway. It was actually a welcome break from the cold.

After cleaning ourselves up we went up to the galley to get some much-needed food. The ship's company had already eaten so we were the only people in the canteen eating. A broadcast came over the tannoy that we were about to get some of the survivors of the Sir Galahad on board for treatment. This was the first we had heard of the attacks on Fitzroy Cove. The chefs told us that a major attack on the ships there had caused an awful lot of deaths. It was about that time when a procession of, what can be best described as walking zombies, began to walk through the canteen to the sick bay. I first thought that their anti-flash gloves were traipsing along the ground off their hand but I realised it was actually skin. When the attack occurred most of them had their sleeves rolled up and the resulting burns were what they were coming to get treated. After the day's event this somehow didn't have the effect on me I would have expected. In normal conditions I would have expected to be horrified whereas all I could think about was getting some food into me. These were truly strange times.

Just before we finished our food the Captain came over the broadcast with a recap of the day's events and he congratulated our team for our efforts and he actually mentioned my name as I was the youngest member of the team, which was nice. Our boss was actually awarded a Mention in Dispatches for leading our team. I had no watch that night and I slept like a baby.'

27

Galahad & Tristram

I firmly believe as I did with the Fearless, the older ships could take the hits, and this proved to be the case with the Plymouth, Glamorgan, Argonaut and a couple of LSLs that received bombs or missiles without being destroyed.

Whilst we were at anchor during this very quiet period, we regularly nipped out for sneaky beakys to drop off various Special Forces through the night. We even had the Ocelot, a submarine, come alongside us one evening for a RAS of fuel and other supplies. It was also to give the 'crabmariners' (submariners) a chance to get off, stretch their legs and have a decent dhobi. And boy did they need it! They don't call them Crabs for nothing. All that time under water with all that diesel and very few opportunities for showers – they really do become very crabby indeed!

The night of the 7th, we were tasked to take the Welsh Guards and Gurkhas around to Bluff Cove to get them nearer to the mountains around Stanley, so they didn't have too far to march over the terrain. The Welsh Guards were not really fit enough to do the full cross-Falklands march (Yomping') as the Royal Marines and (Tabbing)

Paras had been doing. We slipped out of San Carlos under cover of darkness with a couple of Frigates in support to provide cover for us. Nightly excursions were becoming routine for us, and it helped to keep us on our toes during periods of boredom. It was certainly exciting, sailing around the Islands in total darkness. This operation was however complicated by a muddle ashore which meant that the planned rendezvous with Intrepid's four LCUs off Bluff Cove to the east of East Falkland did not occur. We waited longer than planned, hoping the intel we were receiving was accurate, and we were not suddenly going to be attacked by shore based Excocet believed to be deployed south of Port Stanley. Fearless had only two LCUs embarked and thus eventually we could land only half the Welsh Guards battalion, obliged to return the remainder to San Carlos – making the final passage up the Falklands Sound in daylight, a very anxiuous few hours, happily escaping an Argentine air attack in open water.

The next night the two LSLs, Sir Galahlad and Sir Tristram were tasked to deliver the remaining half of the Welsh Guards battalion and various equipment and stores to so they could begin the forward push and support the Royal Marines and Paras who were already on a strong advance forward. Due to loading delays they departed San Carlos later than planned, and arrived at Bluff Cove in daylight. The troops needed to get off those ships as quickly as was humanly possible, as did the Rapier Batterys essential for local air defence. Frustratingly, the Welsh Guards Officer in charge of his troops refused to move his men until suitable transport was provided for his men to move onto their next objective. Major Ewen Southby-Tailyour, who had accompanied the sailing, was livid. As a Major in the Royal Marines, he held senior rank whilst at sea over an equivalent officer in the Army and was equivalent to a Colonel. Sadly, the Welsh Guards Officer refused to accept this piece of protocol and basically told the Major to wind his neck in; he was not moving his troops until transport to his objective was provided. Major Southby-Tailyour was furious and told the Welsh Guards Officer in no uncertain terms that he should get his troops off the ship to prevent a disaster from happening, and he would take no responsibility for what happened to the Guards if he did not disembark his men.

Sadly, the disaster did happen. Argentine observers south of Port Stanley spotted the masts of the two ships sticking out above the low hills. They called in a strike of Skyhawks which duly went in for the kill. The bombs landed bang in the centre of the tank deck of the Galahad, where many of the Welsh Guards were sitting, waiting to go ashore. It was also full of ammunition that needed to be transported ashore for the troops. The explosions were massive and caused many casualties and deaths. The news pictures of these ships exploding are now legendary and demonstrate the amazing skill, talent and bravery of the Royal Navy Helicopter pilots, as they rescued troops from the fo'c'sle and blew the inflatable life rafts away from the burning ships; they flew into black smoke and exploding ammunition to rescue the poor souls from the inferno. If the unloading had started a few hours earlier, as was ordered and ignored, not only would people's lives have been saved, but valuable ammunition and other stores would have been available to the troops.

LCU Foxtrot 4

Foxtrot 4 (F4) was one of Landing Craft Utilities, that sat in the tank deck as we sailed and was used for the main landings. The LCUs could carry a main battle tank, or 4 large vehicles, or 120 troops. She was commanded by a Colour Sergeant, Brian Johnston QGM. He was awarded the Queens Gallentary Medal for his actions in rescuing survivors when HMS Antelope exploded. Losing F4 and her crew was a massive blow to morale and it hit the ship's company badly. One Royal Marine and another member of our ships company did survive and they tried to rescue their shipmates, but to no avail. The crew really had no chance, but revenge was swift when the attacks were witnessed by two Harriers, one of them flown by an RAF pilot, Flt Lt David Morgan, who took 3 of them out and his wingman took out the fourth. It was some consolation that the murdering bastards had not got away with destroying one of our craft.

F4 incident – Leading Radio Operator William Kewn (Scouse to his shipmates)

Scouse reviewed my diary for me prior to publication, and offered to give me his version of the F4 sinking. He had been requisitioned onto MV Monsunnen, a small boat used to transport sheep and other things around the Islands before the War. It had been recovered from the Argentinians, and a team from HMS Fearless manned it to carry out support operations. This incident was to have a profound effect on Scouse's experience of the war.

"As far as I can remember, MV Monsunen was

commandeered shortly after Goose Green was taken. Staff from HMS Fearless were to man it. It was skippered by Lt Ian McLaren RN and his second in command was Sub-Lt Phil Jones (now the First Sea Lord!). There was a Petty Officer Stoker (Engineer), a Killick Seaman, a chef and myself as the Radio Operator. I think I was chosen as I had been trained in naval gunfire support; this meant I was familiar with Army communication methods and also as part of the ship's internal security platoon. The Monsunnen was an inshore coaster which was used by the islanders to transport sheep around the island in the very large hold and here we were, ready to use it to transport the Paras and Gurkhas up and down to Bluff Cove.

It was decided that the safest way of doing it was to transport the troops under cover of nightfall and on return to Goose Green we would camouflage the ship to make it look like a wreck before we got some shuteye.

On the 8th June F4, one of Fearless' LCUs (Landing Craft Utility) arrived astern of us at Goose Green. The Skipper found out that C/Sgt Johnstone, who was in charge of the LCU, was to load his craft up with Land Rovers that were fitted out with hi-tech satellite communications equipment and ferry them to Bluff Cove immediately. We told him that it was too dangerous to do the trip in daylight hours, and that he should wait until the cover of darkness and sail with us, as we were to transport a hold full of Gurkhas that night. He told us that he had his orders and he had to get this consignment to Bluff Cove IMMEDIATELY. They set sail and we waited until it was dark until sailing ourselves.

Halfway into our trip to Bluff Cove we spotted F4 in the

distance and she was stationary. As we got closer we knew there was something wrong; and as we got alongside her I couldn't believe my eyes! I still can't describe the feeling of shock and horror of seeing the back end of the LCU completely blown off. This was where the crew accommodation was and there was no one on board. I just hoped that it was quick and they didn't suffer. I don't think that we had time to even think about what had happened as I think war mode kicked in and there were still Land Rovers with comms equipment intact on board that needed to get to Bluff Cove.

I went on board F4 to tie on a tow rope as we were going to tow it to Bluff Cove. Whilst I was on board F4, I tried getting the ship's plaque for the rest of the squadron but I couldn't prize it free from the bridge. Once the tow was secured I got back on the Monsunnen and we got some of the Gurkhas to play out the rope. As we started moving away, they played out the tow far too quickly and it got completely snagged up around our prop. It snagged so tightly we couldn't move. We were stuck there in the open water still attached to F4! If we couldn't get moving we would be sitting ducks once it got light, we had to cut the tow rope!

We put a cargo net over the back end and a couple of us donned our orange once only suits and took it in turns to climb down and go under water to try and cut through the rope armed only with a bloody bread knife! I don't know how long this went on for but we knew it wasn't working. Just then a frigate appeared in the distance and I grabbed the ship's Aldis Lamp to signal her and tell her of our dire needs. I couldn't believe it; the Aldis didn't work. I had a small right angled torch and started calling the ship but they either couldn't see the light or I was too late signalling them and the look-out didn't see me.

I had a 320 (Army portable HF (high frequency) radio) with me and we needed help. We were under radio silence at the time but I had to break it so that we could get some serious help. I managed to get in touch with a marine somewhere on the island and asked with him to relay a flash message back to Fearless to tell them that we were in desperate need of help. After what seemed a lifetime the frigate I had been trying to call up by light appeared - it was HMS Yarmouth I think; and they came right up alongside us, I thought she was going to crash right into us. They sent down their ship's divers and they cut us loose.

It was nearing daylight now and we knew we would have to turn back to Goose Green with the Gurkhas still on board and the Comms equipment still on F4. As we started back to Goose Green we watched F4 slip slowly under the dark black sea to her watery grave. A prayer was said and I don't think there was a dry eye to be seen. We got back to Goose Green and camouflaged the ship still not believing what we had just been through.

Later that day was when Galahad and Tristram got hit and that is the last thing I remember until we got back to Pompey.

footnote: When I was back on the Fearless on the way home someone told me that the Yarmouth had seen us when I tried calling them, but they thought we were Argies and signalled Fearless to ask them what to do.

I don't know how true it is, but apparently they were

ordered by flash message to engage her guns on us!
Thank God I broke radio silence!'

As always, there were many acts of bravery that day, but sadly many lives were lost or ruined through pure arrogance and ignorance.

28

Chemical Warfare

Wed 9th
*We didn't get attacked but we had a couple of Air
Raid Warning reds calling us to Action Stns, but we
weren't attacked.*
Believed Napalm bombs were used on Galahad.

Thur 10th
*Yet again plenty of Air Raid Reds, but no attacks. They
seem to be bringing every type of A/C they've got out.
Maybe they're planning something because they never
get within 50 miles from us. We have been warned that
there is a huge possibility of gas attacks on us now, so
beards & tashes have to come off. I'm now beginning to
get worried. I don't particularly fancy dying of mustard
gas & being burnt to death by Napalm.*
Not a pleasant thought!

This day was a real psychological shocker to me. We
knew the Argentines had Napalm bombs, as they were
found littered around the airstrip at Goose Green, many in
a very dangerous and unstable state. The enemy appeared
not to take too seriously the safety and maintenance of
munitions. It was reported by many who witnessed

the attacks on the Galahad and Tristram that the bombs released 'rolled' end on end prior to hitting the ships. This was a clear identification of Napalm bombs, as they didn't have the streamlined capacity of the bombs that the Argentines had purchased from the UK and had used to great effect in the war in Bomb Alley.

NAPALM was banned under the Geneva Convention, for use against civilians, in 1980, I believe after the Americans used it to such devastating effect in Vietnam against the Viet Cong and, of course, the people who lived in the villages that the Americans claimed were strongholds of the enemy. Who can ever forget the footage of 8-year-old Kim, running naked, burnt and terrified towards the news camera away from her village, being followed by several other children in similar states? Though, on that occasion, it was a South Vietnamese plane that bombed their own village.

It is a terrifying incendiary, which continues to burn through anything it sticks to. The reason the bombs rolled end on end after being released was due to the liquid/gel inside, which made them unstable. They are an indiscriminate weapon of mass destruction and, when the bomb explodes, the gel is ignited and splattered everywhere, sticking and burning wherever it lands.

The Fearless had taken many survivors from the Galahad incident on board. These were walking wounded that could be treated for their injuries prior to moving on to any further treatment they may need. These poor blokes wandered around the ship with blistered faces, their hands covered in white cream that was put on to protect the burnt skin and then wrapped in plastic bags. They smelled awful, of the smoke and the burnt flesh. It was not a pretty sight and there was nothing we could do.

I was sitting in the dining hall having some scran, when one of the Guardsmen sat down next to me at the table. For a brief moment, I thought I was going to throw up. His hands were puffed up, he had blisters on his arms and on his face, and there was still material in some of the burns. He tried to cut his meal with his knife and fork and kept dropping his knife because he couldn't hold it properly or put any force on it. I leant over and picked his knife up of the tray and just started cutting his meal into small pieces for him. We didn't even exchange words. He was just looking down at his tray. My heart really went out to him, and I felt awful for feeling sick when he first sat down. We didn't talk, he just picked his fork up and starting feeding himself. He looked dreadful and as if he was struggling to eat and swallow the food. He managed it, but his suffering was so visible and I felt deeply sorry for him, suffering as he was. I was still fully intact, warm, calm and alive. Something in him seemed to have died. His eyes showed nothing as he sat there eating his food. He certainly didn't seem to be enjoying it, he was just carrying out a normal everyday function subconsciously, because he had too.

We also had intel that the Argentines were ready to use chemical weapons against us. As part of the NATO Defence Strategy for war with the Russians, all military units and personnel had to be trained in Nuclear, Biological and Chemical Defence (NBCD). This was worked on incredibly hard during exercises at Portland and whenever we worked with other NATO countries. It was something that I never thought I would ever have to deal with.

The training is pretty fierce, with some very graphic footage as what could happen if we ingested any agents. We took this seriously and practised getting our gas masks on within 9 seconds and then checking with your 'oppo' to ensure as much skin as possible was covered by anti-flash or NBCD suits.

The reason for the command to remove all facial hair was that having a beard or moustache would compromise the fit of the Gas Mask, which had to be sealed against the skin. This wasn't a problem for me, because even at 18 I barely had any 'bum fluff' let alone be able to grow a moustache or 'set'!

When you join the Royal Navy, you are taught to shave and would have to shave every day whilst in training. A pointless exercise for many youngsters who joined up at 16 like I did. I rarely shaved daily until this point because I didn't need to; then suddenly it became part of my daily routine. I was not taking any chances! I was genuinely scared at this point in the war and started to wish I wasn't there.

29

Ground War

From this period on, our war was all but over. The fighter wing of the Argentine Air Force had all but been totally destroyed. Air attacks were few and far between now; they had stayed back at base to lick their wounds and probably try to have as much dignity they could muster after the battering they had taken. We mustn't forget that they had caused massive damage to the Task Force when they had attacked us and thrown everything they had at us, and were an amazingly skilled air force. Their pilots were brave and professional during their attacks, and that can never be taken away from them. I believe I speak for the whole Task Force that it was a huge relief psychologically and militarily, because if we continued to suffer the attrition of ships and stores we had in the early days of battle, we would not have been able to fight and achieve what we had set out to achieve; the recovery of the Falkland Islands.

The Royal Navy, the Royal Fleet Auxiliary and Merchant Navy had taken the brunt of the fighting up to this point. We continued to support the ground troops with 'sneaky beakies' at night, but even these were becoming fewer and further between. We could stand down and relax a little, though still be alert throughout the day.

The Army now had to do what Great Britain expected them to do and defeat a force four times larger than them. I don't think the rest of the world expected us to be successful in our efforts!

Most of the tasking of the helicopters that we had - Sea Kings, Wessex, Gazelles and Lynxes was about lifting stores, ammunition and weapons to the front lines. The troops meanwhile had to 'Yomp' (Royal Marines),'Tab' (Paras) and March (Welsh & Scots Guards and any other Army units without the green or maroon beret) the sixty five miles from San Carlos to Port Stanley. Unfortunately, the two Guards units were not fit enough to achieve this, a problem which led more or less directly to the disaster of Sir Galahad and Sir Tristram and the loss of our LCU F4.

This was no mean feat, even with their exceptional fitness training. There were no proper roads, and most of the trek was across hilly and mountainous terrain. Hillocks of tussock grass, pot holes, bogs and rivers had to be crossed, all with at least 100lb of kit to carry. This included their bergans with their personal kit, which was kept to a minimum to make space for extra ammo; mortars, mortar shells, Blowpipe launchers and missiles, GPMGs, belts of ammo for them and their own personal weapons and ammunition. All of this took its toll on a few of them with damaged ankles from hitting the grass wrongly or in potholes. Many of the troops also succumbed to 'Trench Foot', which is caused by the feet being wet and cold all the time, so named because soldiers in the 1st World War, who spent their life in trenches, suffered so badly with this condition. The feet swell and become very painful, making it difficult to walk.

The weather was beginning to turn into icy winter. It changes very quickly on the Islands, one minute glorious sunshine, the next hail or snow storms. The lads also had to bed down at night, dig in for protection and cook up their own grub. 2 Para had already fought the Battle for Goose Green, and were at Fitzroy when the Galahad and Tristram got blown up. They had seen plenty of action, and their next objective was Wireless Ridge, the closest outcrop to Stanley itself. They really had their work cut out.

The most amazing part of this feat was the 'Rock Runs'. These were almost glacier-like rivers of Lime rock which had broken away from the mountains and slipped down into the valleys below. This is nothing like the loose screes around Wasdale in the Lake District, but massive, smooth, generally wet and slippery, blocks of rock, some higher than 6 ft. Imagine having to walk over this with just your normal back pack for a trek up Scafell for the day. These guys had to do this with their full kit they were carrying. And do it they did.

30

What A Team!

In 2007, I was fortunate enough to be invited by Combat Stress to join the Pilgrimage to the Falkland Islands for the 25th Anniversary. This was the first time I set foot on the Islands. On our way (in convoy, by road) from Stanley to San Carlos, we stopped at various points of interest along the way, and this was when I first came across a 'rock run'. I was totally amazed by them and in awe of exactly what the troops had achieved after their long march. Whilst I was in Stanley, I stopped to talk to one of the Paras (Captain Stu Russell) and I said to him "How the hell did you guys achieve what you did? I've seen those Rock Runs, and to 'tab' the distance you did, to carry the kit, get over those runs and still fight and win your objectives... Apart from being incredibly fit, you must have been highly motivated or totally mad!"

"We did it for you guys in San Carlos." came the response. "We spent days sitting on the hillside watching you all get bombed to shit, and we couldn't do anything about it. We were so angry at what was happening, we wanted to pay them back and you guys back also. If it wasn't for you bringing us down here, we would never have been able to do what we had to do and were trained to do. We were all of those things, but at the end of the day we wanted revenge, we wanted revenge for the team!"

As strange as this is going to sound, this was the first time I really understood the meaning of a team. We on the Fearless were a great team and the ships' companies of Sheffield, Coventry and other ships' crews will probably say the same thing about their ships. But it wasn't about individual ships, individual regiments, units, colour of your beret or what badge you wore; it was about all of us being one fighting force as a single team - even the Invisible (HMS Invincible!)

Without each member of our team, as Stu rightly pointed out, we would never have been able to do what we did.

31

Night Terrors

Fri 11th
Yet another quiet day on our behalf, but ashore the Harriers were busy dropping 1,000 lb bombs over Stanley Airfield and other major enemy positions – 25 to be precise, plus missile & cannon fire. Push due to start at 24:00 ('Pongo' time not 'Jacks'!!).

The Royal Artillery and Royal Navy Warships were constantly bombarding Argentine units throughout the day and night with 125mm Guns, and 4.5 shells from the warships. This must have been terrifying enough for the Argentine forces and, if they knew their military history, would have been aware that this was the precursor to an all-out attack.

Somewhere in the annals of time, the military had worked out that we were a much more effective fighting force under the cover of darkness. So, not only had our troops had to put up with the long march across the horrendous terrain, now they had to go into battle in the dark of the night, avoiding the tussock grass, the shell craters and the minefields that the Argentinians had indiscriminately scattered across these beautiful lands.

When people say it's so dark, you can't see your hand in front of your face, they meant it down there! Without the moonlight or starlight, it really is pitch black. Many of the battles were fought almost blind, soldiers relying on the muzzle flashes to locate the enemy. The enemy, although bedded in, would also still have struggled to see at night; sometimes our troops were right on top of them before they realised. Other times, unfortunately, a soldier would step on a mine, losing a foot or leg, and also alerting the enemy that we were on our way.

The Royal Navy never use the term midnight; our operations always begin at 23:59 or 00:01 but never 24:00 or midnight. I believe this helps prevent confusion and, as an ex-matelot, makes sense to me, but the Army works differently and that was the time the Brigade HQ had decided that the battles were going to commence. 24:00 hours. It was a tense time for all as we waited for the countdown to begin.

I never wanted to be in the Army; knowing you are going into battle, hand-to-hand, bayonets drawn, kill or be killed. I have never been able to visualise myself as a fighter or a killer; no matter what amount of training I received I would not have been able to do it.

However, I loved the short time that I had been in the Navy! I had an amount of freedom living away from home but we lived as a group of people and there was always someone to socialise with and watch your back. I was at sea in the early days, in the wilds of the ocean, travelling to exotic places that some of my friends could never have imagined; I had seen the beauty of nature at its most peaceful with the Northern Lights, at its most fun when the Dolphins were racing in the bow wave, leaping and jumping, showing off to us and at its most brutal in hurricane winds that smashed the ship, the waves crashing over the f'oc'sle, troughs deeper than the bridge as we descended into them, and watching a huge wave break above you. It was all very beautiful and dramatic at the same time. I had a warm pit to sleep in every night, hot food 3 times a day, hot showers, good toilets and shelter from the elements. I could also party ashore in foreign climes, find exotic friendly women to spend time with and I got paid for this.

All armed forces have the comradery and some travel; but when the shit hits the fan, the Army in the field have none of the luxuries that we have. This time, they were marching across desolate landscapes, in gales, thrashing rains, hail and snow, permanently wet and damp, sleeping below ground in their trenches, which filled with water, or any piece of shelter they could find. All this with the knowledge that, in a few days, a few hours, they were going to be fighting for their lives but they were fired up and ready, wanting their revenge.

32

The Push

Sat 12th

Push started on time. By 02:00 Mt Longdon was in 3 Para's hands, Two Sisters taken later on in morning. Still fierce fighting going on (13:30). Glamorgan hit by Exocet, but still working & fires are under control. I think she was hit in gas turbine room. Speeding to carriers @ 18kts, so looks promising.

It's very foggy round here at the moment, but are still expecting a huge air attack, either on us or troops ashore. Good buzz we could be on our way home in 3 weeks - but say nowt!!!

Seven Sisters & Mt Longford securely in our hands. 42 took Seven Sisters. 400 odd prisoners taken.

Sun 13th

2nd Para & Scots Guards moved through to take further strongholds nearer Stanley. The Guards had problems but eventually won through with help of Gurkhas (Mt William). Now got all ground. Argies just backed out all over!

The land battles were fast and furious. Our troops had to overcome a force 4 times its size; a force that had been dug in for many weeks in heavily fortified, natural positions, uphill and on the top of mountains. The weather had started turning more and more wintry and it was bitterly cold. After marching for so long, our troops had to fix bayonets, run up mountains, scale rocks, avoid bullets, shell-fire, grenades and kill people, not just with their bayonets, but sometimes bare hands. On Mount Longdon with 3 Para, three young boys were killed in the battle - Privates Ian Scrivens and Jason Burt, were only 17, Private Neil Grose was killed just as he had turned 18 that night. Three plaques sit on Mount Longdon in their memory along with the rest of the names of the men killed.

The Argentinian soldiers apparently included a lot of conscripts, some allegedly as young as sixteen. Many had just left school and were called up/ordered under armed guard; many allegedly did not know where they were going or even where they were when they got there, they were just given some very basic training on how to use a rifle and were put up in the mountains to fight a very professional and motivated army; an army that constantly trained their troops to be the best. Instilled in them was the history and pride of their regiments and units, making them believe in themselves and their mates alongside them. This did not bode well for the conscripts.

On the other hand, there were thousands of professional soldiers who knew how to fight a battle. The officers and leaders of the Argentine army were brutal and had instilled hatred in their men and the passion of what the Falkland Islands (or Malvinas) meant to the pride of the nation. They were a totally different army to ours. It appeared that many of the officers and SNCOs (not all) saw the conscripts as nothing but a bit of shit on the soles of their boots. They were beaten, starved and punished badly for the smallest of things.

A guide on the Falklands told me a story of when he was showing around a group of Argentinians. They came across a field kitchen (still there today 32 years on), and a conscript was amongst the visitors. The conscript explained that all they got to eat was the gravy, grease and fat floating at the top of the stew, if they were lucky. The regulars and SNCOs were given scoops from the bottom of the stew, so they got all the meat and vegetables.

Many of the conscripts gave in to stealing food from wherever they could find it. In Stanley, there were shipping containers full of meats, cheeses, wines, ports, and spirits for the officers, yet these poor, scared, young lads, who didn't understand where they were, why or what they were there to do, were left to almost starve. There is a story of one young conscript, who was caught stealing food; he was tied staked to the ground for twenty four hours in front of his troop. He was left there in the freezing cold, on the mountain side, because desperation of hunger meant he had to steal food just to survive.

This attitude of brutality and the disposability of their conscripts and soldiers was also sadly reflected in how they dealt with their war dead. If ever you have the opportunity of visiting the Islands, and get to visit the Argentine Cemetery, you will find many of the graves are of 'A Soldier Known Only to God.' Each and every one of our dead, including our sailors that went down with their ships, was documented and buried in a marked grave. All that could be moved were reburied at San Carlos, 'Forever a corner of England', and many have since been repatriated to the UK at the request of their families.

The arrogance of the Argentine regime at that time was such that many families do not have an opportunity to visit their fighting men's graves.

Even the number of dead was challenged by the Argentine Government after the war. It was mainly our troops and Padres that ensured those young men's deaths were recorded where they could be (many had no papers or identity on them) and buried in an honourable fashion. If ever people question me about the need for war and freeing the Falkland Islands from a fascist dictatorship, I relay the stories about the graves, the brutality and starvation towards their troops. If they could do this to their own, as well as 'disappear' individuals (thousands), even taking new born babies from their mothers, because they dared to say something derogatory about the regime, just imagine what the people of the Falklands Islands would have gone through.

During the two nights of heavy fighting on the mountains overlooking Stanley, our troops fought with passion and fervour. They fought for themselves and, more importantly, for each other. Those that I have spoken to at various reunions since have always said that if we had been in place for as long as the Argentinians, in the natural shelters and protection that they had, there was no way any force would have been able to remove them. The enemy were so deeply entrenched in their positions and they had great fire arcs for the machine guns and heavier weapons which they used to great effect and killed a good number of our men.

Our men who had marched so hard and still had the will

and the strength to fight and seek revenge for what they had seen, for the pride of our nation and for the pride of their regiments and themselves.

They cleared out sangers and trenches one by one. They took out heavily fortified machine gun positions; they killed men with their bare hands. It was quick and brutal. I say quick, in sense of time, as it only took hours to fight many of the battles. Reinforcements had to be sent into certain areas due to the number of casualties or the strength of the Argentine regiments they were fighting. As a team, regiments combined and fought together for a common goal. The Scots Guards with the Gurkhas climbed the formidable Tumbledown, an awful mountain, but they did it. Two very proud fighting regiments with an amazing military history of bravery and VCs over the years and this was one of the few battles the Gurkhas got involved in, much to their disappointment

Whilst the fighting was going on, we were getting reports back over the net that the Argentinians were getting out of their trenches and walking down the mountains. No white flags, no real panic, just stopping fighting and walking away! It was incredible news, and met with much derision of the Argentine troops by us on board. It was also a massive sense of relief to me and, even as I type this, I can still feel the sensation I felt when I first heard this. It was one of excitement, elation and disbelief. It sounded like it was all over, much quicker than I had ever imagined. I had expected the land battle to take days or even weeks. They had been there for over 2 months, well dug in and fortified and then they literally just gave up. It wasn't just the conscripts either, walking down those mountain sides, streaming towards Stanley. It was the whole force.

The Army was still on alert, the fighting may have stopped in the hills and the enemy were disappearing into the distance, to get away from the ferocity and savagery of the fight to the death, but the officers and artillery in Stanley were still putting out a barrage towards our troops on the mountains. Our lads couldn't relax.

They were also amazed at how quickly the Argentinians had given up. Initially, they were shocked at how hard they had fought against us but, now that the ground troops had all but disappeared, they had to avoid the shells. No one really knew where they were going to land and it must have been hell up there; knowing that they had won a hard-fought battle and then every few seconds hearing a shell whistling towards them.

Sadly, we lost one or two men on the 14th before the White Flags were flown and the surrender announced.

During the night, we upped anchor and sailed out into the dark and the open seas of the South Atlantic to replenish fuel and other stores. This was as dangerous as ever, but gave us a strange view of the land battles.

33

Surrendered

Mon 14th

Did a RAS with Olna. At 04:00 approx, there was a huge air raid over Stanley & Goose Green area. We heard the raid mounting, and had contacts. There were huge flashes of light over the hills which illuminated - (carry on in a mo Captain speaking). Right sorry about that (explain later) - everything. We saw 2 planes get shot down. There was a huge flash in the sky - bigger it seemed than any of the others - which was 1 plane; then we saw 1 burst into flames & spiral down behind the hills on fire. Didn't go to Action Stations, but weren't far off!

Whilst we were out at sea carrying out the RAS, as always, I was on the upper deck, with the signal lantern, talking to the signaller on the other ship and relaying messages back and forth to the commands. Whilst we close in together and get connected it is a very busy time for the RO on the bridge, even more so during a silent transit, and, wherever possible, we were always silent. Captain Larken rarely used voice if he could avoid it, even in peace time. For me this was brilliant! I loved the signalling and our team on the Fearless were probably the best in the fleet.

Ian Napier my 'Sea Dad' encouraged me, generally by 'scudding' me (still does) to read light even quicker and to be fast on the hoists. I was probably transmitting and reading at 12 words per minute, which was the fastest that morse can be read visually. This was great if the person on the receiving end could do this speed, a lot of Matelots couldn't, but the RFA lads had generally served in the RN prior to joining the RFA and were pretty good. I loved it!

We couldn't have been that far off the Islands because I remember clearly hearing aircraft coming in as we were refuelling. The Ops team below in the Ops room kept a close eye on things via the 'plot' as they tracked the aircraft over the sea and headed towards the Islands. We were closed up in Defence Watches, and the Captain was confident that we didn't need to go to full Action Stations.

Being at sea during this stage of the fighting was like watching a black and white film. We could hear the shelling and the bombs exploding as well as see the flashes of light as another bomb/shell landed. It was as black as pitch out at sea, and we could see the fireworks over the Islands. Sometimes there was no sound, as the sky lit up with an explosion, other times I heard aircraft, and then the flash of light and explosion. We watched as planes were taken out of the sky; one was obviously a direct hit and all the munitions on it must have exploded at the same time. A massive fire ball interrupted the darkness of night as a pilot died fighting for 'his country'. Another plane must have had its wings clipped by a ground to air missile; it burst into flames, but came straight down, spiralling towards the ground, fire and smoke trailing behind it, as yet another of the already diminished Argentine Air Force met its demise.

It was a weird scene and a bizarre situation. We were watching a force in its final death throes. An almost third world South American nation, had challenged the might of the third largest military nation in the world, for some desolate piece of land at the bottom of the world, with less than 3,000 inhabitants. Their armed forces were being systematically destroyed by the power and might of the British.

The Argentine Navy had run back to port after the sinking of one ship. They lost one submarine with minimal loss of life, but they were scared to commit what was left of their tiny navy. They even had two ships that were the same as ours, the two Type 42s, one being built in Barrow-in- Furness, and they had the same kit weapons-wise as our two 42s that we had lost – HMS Sheffield and HMS Coventry. We didn't have the option to run and hide; we had to stay and fight no matter what it took. Our force had been severely damaged, with the loss of a number of troops, warships, aircraft and helicopters, but our will was still strong and that was the difference between us and them – we wanted this, we wanted to prove that nobody messes with our Commonwealth, with our people and certainly not with our band of fighting men, which were the best in the world!

This next part of the diary was written during the day. I was writing when the Captain made his pipe, whilst I was settling in my pit for a few hours' kip after the long night I had just had with the RAS, and the excitement of the battles we had just witnessed.

Captain's Speech – At 1552z the Capt made a pipe – "Do you hear there – Captain speaking – You will be pleased to know that the White flag is flying over Stanley!"

There were cheers everywhere! It all started when the CRS (Chief Radio Supervisor) got a message from Args in Stanley (on a net we have for propaganda purposes) - "British Royal Navy, this is Argentine Land forces. We wish to speak to you."

The buzz through the night had proved true! I could scarcely believe it as we heard how they were just running and walking away from their positions in the hills. Our troops had to be told to stop firing at the enemy as they stood up above their trenches and started walking away.

The British had started a propaganda campaign, dropping the inevitable leaflets about how hopeless the fight against a much stronger army was. We were constantly transmitting messages across radio nets that we knew the Argentines were using with the same message. Whatever the reason was that they decided to give up, and I guess it was a whole combination of things, from cold, hunger, low morale, despising their officers and of course the terror of the bombardments, the Paras, the Royal Marines, Scots Guards and of course the legendry Jonny Gurkha screaming down on you, give up they did!

It didn't take long for the message to get out around the ship and I had such a feeling of elation throughout the day, waiting for official confirmation. The Captain made his pipe late in the afternoon. He knew everybody else on the ship knew but, like me, I suspect the rest of the ship's company were waiting for our Captain to tell us the truth. As soon as he made his usual pre-amble, "Do You Hear There, Captain Speaking" the ship went silent, not out of fear and trepidation this time, not waiting for an attack and praying you would survive the attack, but out of excitement and expectation that at last we could

224

finally stand down, lose no more lives and get home safely

As soon as he said the word "White..." the ship was in uproar. I was down in 3 Charlie mess, forward, on the 3rd deck and I could hear the cheers reverberating around the ship. It was an amazing feeling, knowing we had come this far away from home, demolished a force 4 times larger than ours, risked life and limb, lost good strong young men, freed a country from tyranny and had survived.

The Captain, cautious as always, informed us that only the forces on East Falklands had surrendered and that talks were going on for West Falklands to surrender. Although the threat from the air force had diminished, the air force had made no surrender declaration and neither had their navy, not that we were worried about the navy! We still had to remain alert in case of attack, but we were stood down from Action Stations to get some rest. Not that much rest happened. There was too much discussion going on in the mess about everything that had gone on over the past month, how weak the Argies were, what cowards they were, and what a fierce force we were. When are we going home? What happens next?

I felt so incredibly elated, ecstatic and relieved that no more fighting was going on; that no more lives would be lost and that I could go home, knowing I had done my job properly, that we as a ship's company had come together as one and were going home almost intact. I was still concerned about Mac, though we did get updates that he had been transferred to Canberra and was alive. I felt sad for the loss of the men of F4 and their families, but selfishly I also felt happy that I was going to be home with my family and friends in a few weeks from now.

```
O 151212Z JUN 82
FM TPS HEREFORD
TO REDEC/CTF 317
REDFNT/CTG 317.8
REDFNR/CTG 317.0
REDICU/CTG 317.9
INFO REDAPZ/CTU 317.1.1
REDAPZ/CTU 317.1.2
BT
UNCLAS
SIC 19F

HQ LFFI PORT STANLEY. IN PORT STANLEY AT 9 O'CLOCK PM FALKLAND
ISLANDS TIME TONIGHT THE 14 JUNE 1982, MAJOR GENERAL MENENDES
SURRENDERED TO ME ALL THE ARGENTINE ARMED FORCES IN EAST AND WEST
FALKLAND, TOGETHER WITH THEIR IMPEDIMENTA. ARRANGEMENTS ARE IN
HAND TO ASSEMBLE THE MEN FOR RETURN TO ARGENTINA, TO GATHER IN
THEIR ARMS AND EQUIPMENT, AND TO MARK AND MAKE SAFE THEIR MUNITIONS.
THE FALKLAND ISLANDS ARE ONCE MORE UNDER THE GOVERNMENT DESIRED


PAGE 2 REDTUN 002 UNCLAS
BY THEIR INHABITANTS.
GOD SAVE THE QUEEN...
SIGNED JJ MOORE.
MSG ENDS
```

Confirmation Signal to Admiral Fieldhouse

```
     UU
''''ZZ RBDFNT
DE RBDFNR 304 1661307
ZNR UUUUU
Z 151309Z JUN 82
FM CTG CTG 317.1
TO ZEN/HMS INTREPID
ZEN/HMS AVENGER
INFO ZEN/CTC 317.0
RBDFNT/CTG 317.B
ZEN/HMS CARDIFF
BT
UNCLAS
                    INSTRUMENT OF SURRENDER

    I, THE UNDERSIGNED, COMMANDER OF ALL THE ARGENTINE LAND,SEA AND
AIR FORCES IN THE FALKLAND ISLANDS UNCONDITIONALLY SURRENDER TO MAJOR
GENERAL J. J. MOORE CB OBE MC' AS REPRESENTATIVE OF HER BRITTANIC
MAJESTY'S GOVERNMENT.
    UNDER THE TERMS OF THIS SURRENDER ALL ARGENTINIAN PERSONNEL
IN THE FALKLAND ISLANDS ARE TO MUSTER AT ASSEMBLY POINTS WHICH
WILL BE NOMINATED BY GENERAL MOORE AND HAND OVER THEIR ARMS,


PAGE 2 RBDFNR 304 UNCLAS
AMMUNITION, AND ALL OTHER WEAPONS AND WARLIKE EQUIPMENT AS
DIRECTED BY GENERAL MOORE OR APPROPRIATE BRITISH OFFICERS ACTING ON
HIS BEHALF.
    FOLLOWING THE SURRENDER ALL PERSONNEL OF THE ARGENTINIAN
FORCES WILL BE TREATED WITH HONOUR IN ACCORDANCE WITH THE CONDITIONS
SET OUT IN THE GENEVA CONVENTION OF 1949. THEY WILL OBEY ANY
DIRECTIONS CONCERNING MOVEMENT AND IN CONNECTION WITH ACCOMMODATION.
    THIS SURRENDER IS TO BE EFFECTIVE FROM 2359 HOURS ZULU ON 14
JUNE (9 PM HOURS LOCAL) AND INCLUDES THOSE ARGENTINE FORCES
PRESENTLY DEPLOYED IN AND AROUND PORT STANLEY, THOSE OTHERS ON
EAST FALKLAND, LAFONIA, WEST FALKLAND AND ALL THE OUTLYING ISLANDS.


        SIGNED   1. ............... COMMANDER ARGENTINE FORCES

                 2. ............... J. J. MOORE
                                    MAJOR GENERAL
BT



NNNN
```

Copy of surrender doc sent by signal

Nothing much happened between then & now (23:55ish). MGRM Moore went across there, & at 23:30z he should have met General Menendez for yet more talks. Then Capt made his pipe about 2338. He also said that West Falklands have surrendered as well and that the troops were all assembling at Port Howard & leaving Fox Bay – there are approx 1500 blokes.

Intrepid & Avenger are going in tomorrow to collect them. All the Args on East Falkland are now at Stanley Airfield & have laid down all their arms along the road towards the airfield.

If all goes well, troops should start to be airlifted off tomorrow night. Still haven't relaxed though possibility of air attacks still as it's not a total surrender; but not really any problems of dirty tricks from 'Spic Pongo's' because their armies are in a state of disarray.

Our military role really was over now. We listened out for the Captain's pipes, and the buzz coming from the MCO below decks, as to what was happening with the surrender. MGRM Moore eventually got the surrender documents signed and the senior officers and troops under armed guard.

Sadly, a SAS Captain, Captain Hamilton lost his life at Port Howard in West Falkland, when his troop was compromised. He stayed behind to delay the Argies so his men could escape. He was awarded the Military Cross for his actions. The Argentinians buried him where he fell with full military honours. The senior Argentine officer that signed the surrender asked that the SAS officer be awarded an honour, as he was the bravest man that the officer had ever come across. The fight that he put up to save his team and allow them to escape was incredible. He took on a large patrol, was shot and injured on a number of occasions and still carried on fighting to the death.

We still had to get across there and take their surrender and collect their troops and the Intrepid was detailed off to do that. We were required for the Communication to the UK and co-ordination of our Task Group, to pick up and transfer prisoners from various points around the Islands. This suited me fine, as I had really had enough of all the messing around and the battles and was glad that we could relax a bit.

There was no discipline or command of the Argentine forces, who were gathering at Port Stanley, they just seemed to accept it was all over and were wandering around dropping their weapons by the roadside, totally dejected and lost. Our troops took control of everything, gathering them up, building pens for them to stay in so they could be controlled, finding shelter for them such as tents and other materials to keep them warm and providing somewhere to settle.

San Carlos was busy with ships carrying out essential maintenance, relaxing somewhat, but not totally due to Argentina still being in conflict with us. Messages were being flashed all over the place, though many were just ROs catching up and being happy!

Although cold in the South Atlantic, until this day, I could not recall having any heavy snow. The weather changes quickly 'down South' and as the entry states the storm only lasted about 15 minutes, and then all was quiet again.

17 ships in anchorage (Bomb Alley) today. Getting much

colder - we even had a snow storm - lasted about 15 minutes. Stacks of flashing. The buzz seems better now.

The Argentinian Surrender for Land Forces on the Falkland Islands was signed at 21:00 Falkland Island time.

It really was over! The surrender document for the land forces on the Islands was typed up on board Fearless, and was taken away to be signed. The news came through and again cheers and celebration around the ship. It really was the end for us and we could start to look forward to going home at last.

34

Little Man Syndrome

Tue 15th
_All quiet today. Negotiations still going on. GENERAL
MENENDEZ is now a prisoner on board here. He has a
cabin by the Wardroom with 2 armed guards with SMG.
At 14:27 the Union Flag hoisted over Port Howard._

As the senior ship in the area, we 'hosted' Menendez in the
Commanders' cabin. We weren't allowed anywhere near
him and the two Royals with loaded weapons outside the
door ensured he was safe. I was interested to see what he
looked like, and got a glimpse of the little man as I walked
up the passageway. He really was quite short, with jet
black greased hair. It struck me as 'little man syndrome';
Napoleon was short and dumpy, as was Hitler, why did
these immensely powerful men have to prove something
by being so aggressive?

I really did not like the look of him and he fitted the image
I had in my mind from the news reports we had seen
of him on the day of the invasion. He had an arrogance
about him, which also strengthened the mental picture
I had of him in my head being a bully and encouraging
the snobbery and treating of his troops like shit. To this

day, I feel myself getting angry as I recall the image of him in the Commanders' cabin. I know he was a very senior officer, but I felt that he did not deserve such luxury after all the death and destruction he had caused by invading such a beautiful place. In my view, he should have been in the 'brig' at the bows of the ship, freezing his bollocks off and sleeping on a bench. At least he would have been dry, unlike our troops ashore and his bedraggled mob. Our Commander would be able to sleep in his own cabin and have a break. There was nothing to like about this horrible little man!

The hoisting of the Union Flat back in Stanley is well documented. What was really important to me was that it meant that both the main Islands were now back under our control and the people were free but the hoisting of the Union Flag in Port Howard was just as important as real confirmation to the Argentinians that they were defeated.

35

Port Stanley

Wed 16th
Set sail for Port Stanley approx 23:00, but apart from that all very quiet. There was a memorial service at Lympstone for C/SGT Johnson (Killed on the LCU) today 13:00 our time.
Got a maily from Michael (or is it Micheal)

It really was all very quiet. After the chaos that had ensued in the previous weeks and the tension of listening in to what was happening out on the Islands, we really had nothing to do but sail as a normal ship in Defence Watches. The Argentine Air Force had also gone quiet, and were not venturing out of their own airspace. It started to feel like a bit of an anti-climax. As excited as I was that it was over, I was also slightly lost that there were no nerves or anticipation of what next. It was just nothing.

We had word back to the ship that a memorial service for Colour Sergeant Brian Johnson was happening. I'm sure the rest of the crew that were killed were also being remembered and prayed for. It was a sobering thought that this was happening and a gentle reminder of who we had lost.

I don't know why but, whilst I was writing letters home, whenever I wrote to Michael, my future brother-in-law who delayed his marriage plans to Tania whilst I was away, I kept spelling his name as Micheal, much to his amusement. He even reminded me when I got home, that his name was Michael and not 'Michelle', though they did call their first and eldest child Michelle – providence perhaps!

Thur 17th

Arrived Port Stanley at 05:00. Still nothing happening our side. Believe they're mopping up ashore. Got 7 mailys from home. Best morale booster I've ever had & the most letters I've ever received at anytime – stacks of replies to go.

This was the first time I had sight of Port Stanley. We anchored off in William Sound so were a mile or two out of the main port. We could see plenty of movement about Stanley through our binoculars. It looked like the villages in Norway that I'd seen earlier in the year. The bright coloured houses and roofs seemed to go right to the water's edge.

That night there was bit of a riot in town, with some of the prisoners getting a bit hacked off at hanging around, getting cold. Standing on the bridge wing looking out of Stanley, I could see smoke and fires. I thought "Bloody hell, how much more do these poor people have to put with? Wasn't it bad enough they had just been occupied and now these Argy bastards are still giving them hell?"

I never really thought about the welfare or mind-set of the defeated troops. I just expected them to behave peacefully and go home quietly, though they really had nowhere to go, as the Junta back in Argentina didn't want them. It was hardly surprising they were hacked off!

The situation shore-side was getting desperate, there were something like 18,000 Argentinian prisoners around the racecourse in Stanley. Most were stuck out in the open as we didn't have enough tents to go around, thanks to the Exocet attack on the Atlantic Conveyor. Our own food supplies were running low, so there wasn't much for the enemy either. The Junta had disowned these poor men, many of whom had fought hard for their country, losing friends and comrades in the process. It was typical of the regime which we had heard about on board; the senior commanders had no respect whatsoever for their men.

The Brigadier Moore had to send a signal to the Argentinian and British Governments, stating that this was becoming a humanitarian disaster and, if the Argentinians didn't co-operate, we would not accept responsibility for the outcome of these poor men. (Insert signal).

In the days that followed, we sat off Stanley trying to support the repatriation of the Argentine troops by getting them onto LSLs and other ships like the MV Norland to relieve the problems ashore. These men belonged back in their own country but they must have felt even more dejected than they had when they surrendered. Their own government didn't want them, and we certainly didn't. There was no welcome home awaiting them and no honour or recognition for their efforts.

The Yeoman approached me and said that COMAW had put a plan forward for setting up a Queen's Harbour Master to manage the shipping and signal traffic for Port Stanley, whilst the forces rebuilt Stanley and its defences, and he would like me to be part of it with him. The only problem with this would be having to stay down here longer and not go home with the ship. This was exciting; what a thing to be part of. After fighting the biggest seaborne assault since the Second World War, now having responsibility to set up a new control system in Port Stanley. I was a little put out by not going home straight away, but this was soon overcome by the enormity of the potential task ahead, and I wanted to be part of it.

Unfortunately, Woodward stuck his oar in and insisted that as the Senior Naval Officer Afloat (SNOFA) it was his responsibility to do these things, and us little people should wind our necks in. He chose to have his people to do this, and therefore we were stood down. To say I was disappointed was an understatement. The Yeoman also seemed pretty pissed off with us being rejected, however, there was nothing to do but to accept orders from above. Though Fearless did have input into this as the Navigator John Prime did become the first Queens Harbour Master between the period of 14th June - 20th of June when he handed over to Sandy Woodward's man a Commander Hugh Willis RN who had been sent out from the UK!

36

The Dead Zone

Fri 18th
Totally dead.

Sat 19th
Yet again Totally Dead! Andy Maddy took some phots.

Sun 20th
Still very quiet. Life's getting extremely boring and times plodding slowly on. Good buzz going home soon.
S. Thule taken.

Mon 21st
Went to sea at about 0030 to do a RAS with Olna, then anchored at Port San Carlos. We now have 4 ships requisitioned from Args. Monsunen (going back to civvies), Melas Malvinas, Tiger Bay & Yehuin - patrol vessels.
PRINCESS DIANA gave birth to a baby boy.

The immediate period after the war for me was incredibly quiet and difficult. I was still very much alive, and the excitement of what I had just been through had not really subsided. I was kept busy in various ways, but nothing kept my mind as focussed as it had been for the previous month. I was still on edge and high alert. My brain hadn't totally switched off and it wouldn't for a while.

As part of the clean-up operations, and collecting, salvage, the British took responsibility for various patrol boats that the Argentinians had either sailed over in or had 'requisitioned' from the Islanders. Various ships sent skeleton crews across to these small patrol boats (including us as mentioned earlier on Monsoonun) to utilise the boats for supply runs, and transferring prisoners between ships,

South Thule was another island that the Argentinians claimed to be theirs. Like South Georgia, there was nothing on it but an old whaling station. There was no fight for this Island, it was basically a mopping up and admin task which was carried out by the Captains of HMS Yarmouth and HMS Antrim. It was the final chapter of the invasion that needed closing off.

Our new heir to the throne arrived with great fanfare and cheer! I was flying high on being British, being a Royal Navy Sailor that had just achieved one of the most incredible feats ever carried out by the British Armed Forces, and now a new king was born to keep the Monarchy moving forward into the next century. What was there not to be happy about?

Mon 22nd
Dressed ship with Masthead Ensigns for 2nd Heir to the Throne – God Bless Him. Hints of a 'Tot'. Yes, we got our 'Tot' but there was no rum left, so I had to have whisky! Enjoyed it all the same! God Bless the Prince, Princess of Wales & Son!

Saw the home coming of the QE2 on News tonight (ITV News at Ten). It was incredible. I really had to fight back the tears, I had a massive lump in my throat. Didn't see Faz as Kim said, maybe he was on the Beeb – hope to see it. I now feel fantastically proud to be British, I felt proud when we sailed, prouder still when we took Stanley, but today I will never say anything against Britain - I feel fantastic. I hope Mum & Dad come down when we get in.

It is traditional in the Royal Navy to celebrate special events with Dress Ship. When alongside, we hoisted yards of bunting from the fo'c'sle to the quarter deck along the whole length of the middle via the main mast, or masts in our case. It takes a bit of setting up as a bunting and requires the whole team to do it, including climbing the mast to attach additional blocks to hoist the bunting up the yardarm. It looks good and attractive, and creates great photo opportunities from shore!

When we are at sea, we dress with Masthead Ensigns. These are larger Ensigns than we would normally fly whilst at sea, and really make the ship look proud. The fact that we had Ensigns flying from wherever we could whilst we were in Bomb Alley meant that the ship didn't really look that different. Though now we were out in public again, and we had the 'Gold' sniffing around.

The issue of the Tot was also a traditional celebration for the Royal Navy. It used to be a daily ration of rum until 1971 when it was scrapped for various reasons, which included that warships were becoming more technical and the sailors had to be more professional and proficient to operate them. Half a pint of rum a day probably was not the best idea! So, the Tot was replaced with the '3 cans per

239

day per man perhaps!' I had never officially had a Tot of rum - save as for HMS Victory, and how traditional was that. I had only just turned 18, so I was really looking forward to it. It was being issued from the Wardroom Cabin flat in the traditional way, out of a Tot barrel. By the time I got relieved to go off watch, the barrel was empty, and the Joss Man was pouring out Bells Whisky instead! Hey it was a spirit which you didn't get on board as a rating, so I made the most of it and most welcome it was too.

By now we were getting regular flights with stores, mail and news (we didn't have satellite in those days, though we did have video players on the ships) being delivered to the ships. We were starting to get a feel about how the country was viewing our achievements down here. We thought it was brilliant leaving, but what we were seeing in letters from friends and family was indicating that coming home was going to be incredible. My sister had written to me to tell me that Faz had arrived back in Southampton on the QE2 with the other survivors from the various ships. One of the videos we received was of her homecoming.

Watching the crowds and the flotillas going out to meet her, as she sailed into Southampton, was one of the most emotional things I had ever seen. It would appear many in the mess felt the same and there were many excuses about it being smoky in the mess (we were issued with 200 cigarettes and allowed to smoke in the mess decks back then). The comments from all of us ranged from 'F***ing hell', 'Amazing, though those poor blokes need it' to "I don't want any of that crap. Just want to get home and get on with it." And various other incarnations in between. What we did know by this was that we were being hailed as conquering heroes and deep down I really wanted to get

240

home to a welcome like that. Even today, I can feel exactly as I did back then in the mess. I can see us all standing around the telly, the goose bumps creeping over my body, tears welling in my eyes, but not spilling, wishing I was them and my Mum and Dad would be on the dockside waiting to greet me with open arms. It was a feeling of pride and hope that things were going to be alright.

Wed 23rd
Still nothing happening. Talk of going home tomorrow. Di takes baby home.

We had been given a date to sail for home, but this kept changing. Another buzz around the ship was that we were definitely going home the next day. I didn't hold my breath!

37

FOSA – Flag Officer South Africa

Thurs 24th

Should have sailed at 1000z, but as usual the ship's always late. FOF1 wasn't happy with the situation down here (but he wouldn't be, he's never been here. FOSA – Flag Officer South Africa – good buzz they had a run ashore in South Africa!) until today; sitting pretty in his prima Donna carrier, so he came down & we eventually sailed 12.5 hours late 22:30z. CLFFI & CinCfleet had told us to get troops home etc. (HQ sig sqdns, RM, Blues & Royals - nice!), 846 Air Sqdn & Fleet Clearance Diving Team, but FOSA probably wanted to be the first big ship home, for the glory.

COMAW (Commodore Clapp) left the ship today to go to the Bedivere, so we're no longer Amphibious Flag Officer. Bill Byrne also went on Bedivere. RFA Sir Galahad taken out & sunk now designated a war grave, our 5th one out here. First landing of a Hercules at Stanley Airport today. I think it had the Governor Rex Hunt on, it did an air drop over Stanley first.

YEHUIN renamed FALKLAND SOUND.

There was still a lot of animosity towards the carriers, even now the war was over. They were still taking the glory for the victory, and still getting most of the freebies that were being sent out, as far as we were concerned. Admiral Woodward coming over for a handover and check what was going on was just another added pain in the arse that we didn't really need. We were bored. We had won the war and now we wanted to get home.

I think, in the end, the intervention of the CLFFI - Major General Moore, who needed to start getting the soldiers back home and CinCFleet Admiral Fieldhouse, the Task Force Commander who of course held a higher rank than Rear Admiral Woodward, detailed off a few troops to board and ordered us home. The Admiral didn't turn up! The moment couldn't come soon enough for me and, 12 and a half hours late, we set sail away from the Falkland Islands having done our job, with pride and honour.

Every one of us on board that ship that day including the embarked forces had all fought hard, dealt with deadly situations, saved lives and ships and liberated a country. We had a good mix of troops with us and a very relaxed, happy atmosphere as we steamed north.

My best mate Bill Byrne went off with COMAW to support his communications team, and stayed a few extra weeks on or around the Islands. He thought he would be flying back into Brize but he joined us for our trip back into Portsmouth for the homecoming. It wouldn't have seemed right without Bill being there.

The Galahad could not be salvaged, and was still smouldering this far on from the dreadful day of 8th June. The souls of the men that could not be rescued, and had died on the ship, remained on board her as she was towed out to sea and discreetly sunk with the minimum of fuss. It was a dignified end for those poor men, as their bodies were committed to Davey Jones' Locker and stayed forever on patrol.

Sir Rex Hunt returned home in style and was warmly welcomed by 'his' Islanders to set about the mammoth task of rebuilding their lives, and making the beautiful Islands of the Falklands safe again.

After the surrender, we were horrified to discover that the Argentinians had indiscriminately scattered mines all over the place. They rarely recorded where they had planted these anti-personnel and vehicle mines, and our troops had to set about making sure areas were fenced off and started defusing them. There was lots of joking about sending the sheep out across the hills to detonate them without us losing any men. I don't think it would have been a goer, but it was a good laugh for many of us to imagine them popping off and becoming instant pot mess!

38

Homeward Bound

Fri 25th

Another day just beginning (00:20) & we're at sea
HOMEWARD BOUND!

Went into NBCD state 2 condition Y at 07:25, then about half an hour later state 3Y. Left the TEZ at 09:40z steaming at 16 knots. State 3X at 0913z just as I turned in. Now 1 in 4 watches. Had head down until about 11:45 then got woken by someone in the mess shouting. Got up went on watch at 16:00 & off at 1800, reported the mess for rounds after clearing it up; reported rounds in slippers as my steaming boots have gone missing. Turned in again at 20:30 and was woken yet again at about 23:45 by the same person. It's getting beyond a joke now – they're all so ignorant down here.
Apart from that the day's gone without incident.

What a relief! We had set sail just before midnight and were now on our way home. I had the long middle/up all night. Part of our planning for action is to shut down the ship to ensure water tightness, fire protection and boundaries. For over a month, we were in NBCD State 1Z. This is when all the hatches are closed, the kidney hatches have to be shut (small hatches in the middle of the larger ones for escape). As we got further north, we relaxed to State 2 condition Y, which meant more hatches could be opened and then finally State 3X which was peacetime cruising. We were there!

We also relaxed from Defence Watches to resume normal cruising watches, which are 4 hours on, 8 hours off, and variations of time on watch in between. Having been up all night, and in desperate need of sleep, with the excitement finally wearing off, I was in a deep sleep, when suddenly a loud bang woke me, as the mess door flung open I heard the screeching voice of the little LRO Tom Sawyer! I was still on edge, so the banging door scared the shit out of me; the combination of this and his high pitch, squeaky voice and realisation that it was just him pissing around, meant I woke in a foul mood. He didn't give a toss about others and thought it funny to wake us all up. Tom was a 3 badge Killick (possibly Long Service & Good Conduct medal – fifteen years minimum), so we had to be careful with what we said to him.

People were really starting to get to me, and wind me up. There was no rhyme nor reason to it, it was just how I felt. I got wound up very easily, which was unusual for me as I was always quiet and avoided confrontation as much as I could. I wasn't impressed though when I came back into the mess to get dressed to report rounds and some idiot had taken my steaming bats out and hidden them somewhere. In normal circumstances it would be funny but, trust me, this wasn't normal. The way I was feeling wasn't normal and I was bloody pissed off!

Sat 26th
00:45 still awake – if he didn't have a hook on his arm

246

I'd plant him one. 18 days to crack and counting! Totally dead today, only 2.5 thousand miles of Ascension at end of day. Fired off 3 in rockets. Good Night!

Tom was behaving in his normal obnoxious mode. He did have an anchor on his arm, which made him a Leading Hand and me just an RO. Our mess in 3C1 was a small mess, and probably the best located mess on the ship, it had fifteen bunks 3 up around the bulkheads and the lockers were in the middle, like a dividing wall. Tom slept around the back in the 'Killick's Gulch'. I was in the middle set on the bottom pit, which also doubled as a seating area to watch the telly.

It really upset me at how he behaved during that short period. For over a month, we rarely saw each other due to the watches we were keeping, Action Stations and anything else that was thrown at us. When we were allowed to get our heads down during the war, everybody did. I was too knackered not to, and I knew I had to sleep, the transit through the TEZ and into Bomb Alley proved that to me. I know I had been up and about for nearly 2 days with very little sleep and I coped with it probably due to the adrenalin, but I was totally shot after that. Whenever I could, I would grab 30 minutes here or there. Just after raids, and we were given the all clear, a quick head down in the VS store prior to the next raid became a godsend!

Now this annoying idiot was being a real pain and I could do nothing about it. Saying something would just encourage him further because he would know he was winding me up. I had to hold my tongue and do the best I could to get sleep. I'm sure we were all dealing with the quiet and what we had just been through in our own way.

Mine was to shut down, and keep myself to myself. I just wanted to relax. Tom was a ball of high energy and he made sure everyone knew it!

The days-to-go chart had started and I was ticking it down one by one. I had decided that I would keep the diary going until we actually got alongside. The war wasn't properly over for me until I was safely back in England and on dry land.

Sun 27th
Had a memorial service for those lost in F4 today, an emotional experience, but then what can you expect when they're blokes we've all worked with.
Apart from that another quiet day. Had a call round to Mac's Mess, had a few tinnies watched Enter the Dragon (Bruce Lee), came back down the mess at 22:30 (ish) had another tinny & the Commander came down to borrow a mag from one of the Lads. I nearly died, 'coz you're not allowed to drink after pipe down 22:30, but I don't think he saw me. Got the middle 23:55 - 04:00, crack a maily home to Paula. I think it'll probably be the last one 'coz only 17 days (nearly 16 days) to go. Changed back to sheets instead of sleeping bag 'coz it's getting warm - nearly 10Degs C now, a rise of 8 or 9 since we left Stanley - soon be bronzy weather.

It was only right that, as things quietened down, we remembered our fallen. I remember my mood being very sombre through the day.

A 'call round' is an invite to another mess to share the beer ration. It usually ends up quite a boozy affair! In those days, I could drink a fair bit and still behave in a reasonably normal manner. It was good to be able to relax and catch up with each other and we made the most of it.

When I returned to my own mess, the fridge was still open and most of the mess up and about and drinking. I decided to have a night cap and, just as I opened the tin, in walked the Commander. I thought he was doing rounds to ensure that everything was as it should be. Instead he came down to borrow some dodgy mag, from one of the older blokes in the mess! Officially this type of material was banned on Royal Navy Warships but it was difficult to manage. By today's standards what was available was pretty tame, and I don't suppose Penthouse was that outrageous! All I could think about was being trooped if I got caught drinking out of hours but it was ignored as the swaps took place.

Writing home was still part of the daily routine for me. Once we got to Ascension that possibly would be the last time the mail would go off. We may have had Gib as we steamed past or in the Western Approaches of Cornwall, though by then we would only be twenty four hours or less from home. It felt great to be able to write to someone who I thought was the one and we could rekindle what we had the year before. I was beginning to wind down; and sliding into crisp cotton sheets, after living in or on a sleeping bag for months, was a luxury.

April 6th Leaving Portsmouth

Harrier and Sea King

Antelope mast bent and bomb entry hole visible

HMS Plymouth bombs missed

One Half Tactical Comms Dept (Kevin in White Artic Rig)

Phew that was close!

Spot the low flying aircraft

Arriving home

A mum's welcome for Millom's Falklands hero—see Page 3

39

Thank You Sand Bags!

Mon 28th

15 days to go. Get in on 14th now. Took the sand bags from the front of the bridge to find one of the bridge windows shattered where it had been hit. Still quiet. Didn't crack any mailies.

The date for our arrival home had been set. We knew now, just as we did when we set sail south, there was no turning back, we were steaming North and home!

We started to really clear up now and the de-sandbagging was continuing at a pace. The bridge on the Fearless is raised and there is a walk-around passage between the command console and the outside of the ship. We would stand in there as lookouts in peace time during wet or wintry/cold conditions. During the war, we filled this area with sandbags, as we did the bridge roof around the GDP. It was a good job we did. As we were clearing the bags, we discovered one of the windows had been smashed, if there wasn't the protection of the sand bags, the shrapnel could have penetrated and killed or injured people on the bridge. When we cleared the sandbags from the bridge roof, Starboard side above the RO's consul, we discovered

2 unexploded rockets embedded deep into the sandbags. There may have been a heavier load of extra ballast on the ship with all the sandbags, but there is no doubt that the Captains idea and desire to protect the key operational areas of the ship saved lives. If the bags hadn't been in place on the roof, the whole bridge area could have been destroyed as well as the guns on either side potentially suffering some serious damage. The rockets were carefully passed down and then dropped over the ship's side into the depths of the Southern Ocean.

Finding these munitions so close to where I operated really set my heart racing. In my mind I could see the damage, and I imagined what I would have looked like if I had been caught in the explosions and not killed. How would I have coped if I had been injured by one of these things, or how would my Mum and my family live after I had been killed? It really scared me; I had thought that after what I had just survived I couldn't be scared again, that my war was over. Little did I know that my war was not going to be over for many years to come.

Tues 29th
15 days to crack. Wrote a maily home during the morning watch, but I haven't posted it yet. Watched the Spy Who Loved Me – got a flash of Fearless. All night in tonight.

Wed 30th
Saw some flying fish for the first time on return journey. Turned too up top to do some painting. It's now bronzy weather, but still a bit windy, but caught some sun today. Did PT as well – God! It was murder! But must get rid of me fat tum, so stacks of sit ups & trunk curls done tonight. 70 whilst on watch and 30 between 1630

- 1700 & I'm knackered.

R/V with Southampton to transfer stores & her mail. Had to go right of course for her delaying us further. A couple of ciggies by light & left her about 2345 & we're on our own again. Apart from that all quiet.

14 days to go. Did RAS with British ESK - a BP tanker. This month has flown by, I only hope the next 2 wks do as well. Must remember Fleet Form 3.

40

Preparing For Home

Thurs 1st July
13 days. Had machinery breakdown in the afternoon, delaying us slightly, but got it sorted out in an hour or so. Just over a day to go to Asc. Weather's a bit rough but not too bad, windy but warm. We are now going into Pompey with Intrepid & her leading would you believe?

Every hour was of the utmost importance to me for our transit home. I started to get really frustrated with things like a RAS and changing course; machinery breakdowns were a worrying thing, as we could be left floating around for ages until the problem was fixed. Like every department on board HMS Fearless, the Stokers were probably at their best. Just like me I expect, they did not want any delays in getting back home and they were on the ball to resolve any problems.

This part of the transit was incredibly quiet. It had been a long time since we sailed alone. The peace and quiet was almost unbearable, but I soon got used to it. As we transited further north, the change in the weather was very noticeable. I couldn't wait to feel the hot sun on my face again, and start to get some colour back into my body.

I felt that I had hidden my body away from the air for far too long, and need to get those UV rays back on it!

The Fleet Form 3 is a security pass for friends and families. We needed to send them home to complete and bring with them to get access into the Dockyard or any other Naval Establishment you were serving at. I had to make sure that I sent them home, and not miss the mail at Ascension, if I wanted my family to be there when I got back.

I did write to tell them that it probably wasn't worth coming down because I wouldn't be home that weekend as I was on duty. We were giving the 'RAs' (Resident Ashore), commonly known as married and generally with children, the advanced leave and 1st weekend so they could get home and spend time with them. What was another week for me? I would be alongside in Pompey, would have spoken to all my family at some point that week and then would be heading for home the following weekend - no hardship. Still, it wasn't up to me to decide if Mum and Dad were coming down, they would make their own mind up and no way was I going to be able to influence them.

The audacity of it all! HMS Intrepid leading us back into Portsmouth. How dare they! We were the Command ship in the Amphibious Zone and we should be the ones that went in first! The rivalry was still there and it was almost hostile at this stage in the proceedings. There was a feeling amongst many that Captain Dingemans who had higher seniority than Captain Larken and had pulled this seniority on us when the Command were organising the return. I was not impressed and I don't think many others were either. It didn't really matter a toss looking back on it, but at the time! However, whilst in conversation with Captain Larken, I later discovered that he himself had suggested the Intrepid lead us in, as we had already had 'the bulk of glory' from the war, and therefore felt that it would give the Intrepid's Captain and crew a bit of a boost to be the lead ship. He was anxious also not to impose excessive wear on Fearless's propulsion on the run home – the ship had several years to run, whilst Intrepid was to go directly into operational reserve.

Fri 2nd
12 days to go. Still moving and getting warmer. Got over flown by Nimrod which circled a couple of times, & later by a Phantom which did the same. Helo from Asc arrived with mail.

41

Red Cross Parcels

Sat 3rd

Got mail about 01:00, but didn't get any in 1st collection. Got some in second though. Reached Ascension about 03:00, went alongside ALvega for RAS (L). Got 2 nutty parcels about 06:00 – I didn't think they'd arrived yet. The one from Tania and Michael & the one from the people in the street. I couldn't believe it when I read who it was from; I felt really weird. It was unbelievable especially the box of Fruit Gums from Johnny and Caroline.

Got 2 more big parcels later on during the morning – 1 from Mum & Dad & one from the girls. The lads were really chuffed & there was plenty to go around for all, with stacks spare. Locker's full of nutty & we have a box of nutty in the fridge for us all. My cake's in there as well, hope it keeps 'coz it'll be a while before I get to it. Left Asc about 13:00ish. 11 days left.

In my letters I had received in previous drops, the family kept me updated on what was being shown on the news or what they had sent out to me, so when the videos arrived and were played on board, I got a chance to catch up.

I didn't expect what I got on this day! I don't think the rest of the ship's company did either! Anchoring off Ascension to replenish with fresh stores and mail was a great feeling. It was hot and sticky again and we were at the half way stage heading in the right direction.

It was also a time for the stores and admin ashore to catch up with everything they had missed or waited for as our ship got closer. There were several mail drops this day. One load actually dropped a mail bag, and parcels and letters were blowing everywhere on the flight deck. We had the supply blokes to help bring in all the bags and other stores that were filling our decks! I got four 'red cross' parcels that day, from my family, neighbours and the people of Millom. The girls at Elbeo had collected stuff for me which included razors, toothpaste, deodorants, sweets and other necessities. I had a big cake sent to me, with shed loads of 'nutty'. It was like Christmas ten times over!

What really got me was the parcel from Market Street. Friends and neighbours had filled a box with all sorts. Silly joke gifts including a 'Break Glass In Nuclear Emergency' set, which contained a single cigarette, an aspirin, a plaster and a tea bag! It was stuck on my 'buggery board' for years on all the ships I served on. Yet even more amazing was a box of Fruit Gums from Jonny Murning and Caroline Moore. They were only about 6 years old at the time. Jonny had a problem with his spine and was constantly in a brace; he was one of the cutest, cheekiest little chappies you could meet. Attached to the box of Fruit Gums was a 20p piece with a little note on it saying that they had some change left from their pocket money and wanted me to spend it. I was choked then and still am! It was one of the sweetest things I had ever encountered and really showed how much people thought of me, and of course everybody else in the Task Force.

3 Charlie was awash with boxes of nutty, cakes, fizz, cigarettes, toiletries and whatever else. The NAAFI would soon be out of business at this rate. We left boxes out on the fridge and cakes inside the fridge, so we could help ourselves as we went along. 'Naps' rightly decided that we should save stuff for the kids and families when they came on board in Pompey, and so we stowed a load away in various cupboards and lockers. This demonstration of care and warmth towards us was a highlight of the war and everything that was good about people and the British for me.

12 hours later we were on the move and in the final stretch. I really did not mind this delay on this day. I was on a high, and not just from the sugar rush!

Sun 4th

10 more days. Stacks of 'Bronzy Bronzy' weather, tan's coming along nicely. Crossed Equator at about 1900 or thereabouts. Nothing exiting. Saw the news with us on, that I think must have been what Mum was on about. Saw Gregory's Girl - great film!

42

Pulled Out His Plums

Sun 11th

A week gone by & it's been dead, had a 'country fair' in aid of F4 and raised over £6,000 - £300 of that being paid for a chocolate cake! We've had a RAS (L) with Plumleaf & rendezvous'd with Brilliant. Stacks of painting. Tried for 3 days to get through to Kim on Radphone calls - no joy.

It's traditional in the armed forces for the deceased's kit to be auctioned off, to raise some money for their family. Being on board, we were able to do a lot more. We had plenty of R & R on the way back, ate loads, drank loads and basically chilled out and got a lot of the excitement out of the system. Today was a day for the whole ship's company and our last few embarked guests (we unloaded a few troops off at Ascension and they would be flying home), to have bit of a party and raise some cash.

A country fair was arranged, with all sorts of stalls and amusements. Matelots are very creative when they need to be; one of the best being the Human One-Armed Bandit. 4 blokes in a row, 3 with a sack in front of each of them, the fourth one stood with his arm in the air. You paid your pound and pulled his arm down. The 3 blokes made daft noises of a mechanical nature and pulled out their plums, apples, bells or cherries, if they hadn't lost it. If you had a match you won a prize tinnie and then had to pay another quid for the privilege!

All sorts of attractions were happening that day, including a 'Miss Fearless' competition. How, you may ask, can we have a 'Miss...' anything competition three thousand miles out at sea with no women on board, and on our victorious journey home from war. I've already said how innovative sailors and other servicemen are, and boy did we have some innovation and imagination for this! The outfits, underwear, wigs and makeup that appeared to create this beautiful spectacle, were nothing short of miraculous. There were some very beautiful looking young 'ladies' on that flight deck (and no, not just because I'd been at sea nearly 100 days).

The contestants were attended by their 'people' to ensure they looked the most beautiful. They paraded around in a circle, sashaying seductively, trying to look as sexy as they could, with wolf whistles and cat calls of various abusive styles being hurled at them as they lined up, prior to being interviewed by The Master of Ceremonies, our very own Captain Jeremy Larken! Some of these guys had the charm to charm the pants of you in 30 seconds flat. They were judged by a panel made up of various members of the ship's company, who judged them on their style, their looks (I think) and the quality of answers given, not forgetting the wolf whistles and cheers.

There was a fantastic BBQ with great steaks (massive great steaks) and various other pieces of meat, salads etc., copious tins of beer were consumed (relaxed watch keeping as well), and we all had fun as a ship's company for the first time in many months.

As relaxed and fun as it was, the serious business of raising money for the bereaved families soon began. It started harmlessly enough, with things like books, shoe brushes, dusters and other bits of kit that the lads had in their lockers. A small item of clothing like a pair of boxer shorts would sell for £50.00 and, as the auction moved on and people became more relaxed, the bidding prices rose with each item. The chefs had cooked a beautiful looking chocolate cake, which was auctioned on behalf of our lost comrades. A consortium of Senior Rates and RM SNCOs/NCOs, drove the bidding into a frenzy. The price kept rising as the different messes and Wardroom tried to outbid each other. Remember this was 1982. I was paid £80.00 a week and I watched and listened aghast as the price for the cake eventually reached its peak and the hammer came down at £300.00! Just under 1 month salary for me! It was out of this world, knowing that people cared so much and were so generous for those families. It would be little consolation to them without their son, brother or husband any more, but I hope it helped them to know how warmly we felt and cared about them and their loss.

As we got closer to the UK we were allowed to make calls home by booking through the main communications office, and, as ROs, we got a little bit of slack and were able to 'jump the queue'. I tried to get hold of my sister for the first time since I left her in early April. Why I never called home, I don't know, I don't think we had a phone in the house at the time. I tried desperately without any success to get through to her. The phone just kept ringing and ringing; it was so frustrating. I just wanted to hear her voice and talk about me coming home and tell her that it wouldn't be worth Mum and Dad coming down because I wouldn't be home that weekend as I was going to be on duty. I wanted to tell her anything, just to hear her voice again, to be connected with home again.

It wasn't to be, and though disappointed, I knew we would be home in 3 days! We were sailing into Plymouth first with HMS Brilliant, who was based there, and to drop off the Royal Marines and any other troops we had left. After that, we would make full speed to Portsmouth overnight, to rendezvous with HMS Intrepid prior to her leading us into our berths in the Royal Dockyard.

43

Home Waters in Guzz

Mon 12th

2 days left. We were off Plymouth sometime during the first. We could have dropped the troops off and been home by tomorrow afternoon.

Tues 13th

Anchored or rather secured at C Buoy in Plymouth Sound. About 0630, started unloading troops. There were loads of small boats & ferries coming out to meet us during the day all waving and cheering.
Brilliant came in.

We stayed secured to the buoy through the night. It was always frustrating anchoring or doing circuits just a few miles off shore overnight as you could see all the comings and goings shore-side and sometimes even hear the music and people having fun ashore. Imagine what it was like so close to home after ninety eight days at sea!

Well what a welcome! As dawn broke, in fact even through the night, small boats were coming out to us, cheering and flashing their lights. Once daylight arrived, it was hectic. There were hundreds of small craft and ferries sailing out to greet us and some escorting the LCUs into the breakwater and getting the Royals ashore. There was every craft you could imagine, some with bevvies of beauties treating us to eyefuls of all that was beautiful! They weren't just there for us of course. HMS Brilliant was coming into her home port also, and she was greeted equally as passionately and made her way into the harbour escorted by two tugs, firing the fire hoses in the air as they led her in. It was a 'Brilliant' sight (pun intended - no other words) to see and feel.

As exciting and thrilling as all this was we still had a job to do, not least welcoming the Duke of Edinburgh on board as the General Commandant of the Royal Marines, who came on to shake everybody's hands and welcome his Royals home. It was a great honour for all of us to have this level of Royalty on board. We couldn't expect Her Majesty as we knew she was saving her love for her heroic son, who made like an Exocet decoy on many occasions. I don't know the truth because I was more than 50 miles away in the middle of a war, dodging shells, rockets, bullets and aircraft falling out of the sky!

The Duke's visit, as illustrious as it was, really didn't mean as much to me as it probably should have done as I look back on the day. It was great he was on board and that his Colours were flying from the main mast, and only right and proper that he should come to welcome his troops. Truly I felt honoured and proud, but only briefly. I was too interested in what was below us on the water and the reception we were getting from the hundreds of boats bobbing about in Plymouth Sound. Neither the noise nor the crowds seemed to let up, and I really, really wanted to get home now. Another twenty four hours and the war would finally be all over for me!

44

The Glorious Day

Wed 14th

The Glorious Day at long last. Anchored at Outer Spit Buoy about 0700 (ish). Boats started appearing like yesterday. Made our way in & there were thousands & thousands of people to greet us - it was fantastic, none of us could believe it, it was very emotional & the proudest day of my life!

Well that's the lot 'thank God' & now I can believe it's all over, 'coz we're home. So here ends my summary of events (diary even) of the Falklands Crisis.

I couldn't sleep through the night, nor did many others in the mess. Tonight though I was happy that everyone was in such a party mood. The animosity of the early days of our departure from the war had largely disappeared, tonight was about celebration, talking about what was to come and saying goodbye to shipmates who had been drafted on specifically to go to war with us. A channel night was had, as we made our way from Plymouth to Portsmouth. This was a night where we have a final piss up before getting alongside to our wives and girlfriends and the drinking activities get curtailed!

Traditional naval songs are sung, games like Ukkers 'An immature adult game of Ludo played by Sailors' as quoted in the Oxford English Dictionary, and spoons are played. Spoons is a mad game, where one of the sprogs of the mess takes on an old salt in trying to smash each other on the head, with a spoon gripped by the tip of the handle between your teeth. The players sit opposite each other and take it in turns to bring the spoon down as hard as they can. It is very difficult to hurt anybody in this way, but the old salt can really smash that spoon down hard, especially as his oppo is standing behind the sprog with a ladle or other such implement; after a few hits from the small spoon it starts building up with a couple of taps with the heavier ladle, and then whack! The sprog doesn't stand a chance much to the amusement of the crowd and his 'Team in the corner'!

As we sailed up the Solent between the Forts, the IOW and Portsmouth, in the grey blue early morning light, we could see crowds forming along the sea front. Cars were flashing their headlights in our direction, and guess what, boats, yachts and dinghies, hundreds of them, were sailing out to greet us. The excitement and happiness was almost overwhelming. As we went to anchor, and yes, I was the 'Bunting' on the fo'c'sle, with the flags, indicating how many cables the chain had gone down, I was like a small child who had just woken up at Christmas with a big tree surrounded by presents. I was buzzing!

The shackle was released from the anchor chain by the deck party and as it clattered and clanked loudly, being dragged at a great rate of knots to the murky, depths of the Solent, I hoisted the Union Jack as smartly and quickly as I could without any hitches; after all, I had an audience of well-wishers watching my every move. I wanted to make sure that our ship and our crew looked like the well-drilled fighting force of sailors that we were. I'm sure they didn't give a damn about the ceremonial aspect, or knew how much it meant to me that I got this looking smart and correct; besides the CCY would have bollocked me if I didn't! I secretly enjoyed this part of the job, but let the others know that it really pissed me off so they would continue to make me do it! Today was going to be a special day for me; I had to do Cable party.

I secured the halyard to the Jack Stay and promptly grabbed the appropriate numbered pennant to signal to the bridge how far the cable had dropped. I was floating on cloud nine. I don't know how I managed to concentrate at all that day; all I wanted was to be alongside and back in the safe and comforting arms of my family.

We had to anchor to release the 3 LCUs, who had a lonely trip back with the empty berth that was F4. Even though we had only been on the ship together as a crew for 9 months, the emptiness of that tank deck was a bleak and sad reminder of what we had lost. I felt sorrow at the blank space and avoided the quarter deck as much as possible so I didn't have to see it. For the crew of the other 3 LCUs it must have been so difficult for them to work down there on a daily basis and, today of all days, to sail out of the back without their comrades and ship mates; what a terrible mix of emotions would have been going through their heads and hearts.

As the LCUs were floated out, I secured the Cable Flags returning them to their correct stowage on the bridge wings. One final last scrub of the ship, to make it look as smart as possible for the crowds that were about to deluge us, and then down for a hearty breakfast, and into the mess to get into my No 1s for Procedure Alpha and our triumphant return into Portsmouth!

The noise from the flotilla of boats was incredible as we weighed anchor. The hooters, the shouts of 'Welcome Home!' and the cheers that were ringing all around us were like a great cacophony of joyful sound. Many of the craft had large Union flags and Ensigns, some tied to their masts, others to beautiful young ladies with sometimes very little else on. What a welcome and we hadn't even got alongside. What was to come was even better!

We raised anchor and set sail in Formation 1 with Intrepid as the guide ship. We had our Falklands Campaign Flag that was designed by the Yeomans George Mellor & George Moutter, and sewn together by the team, hoisted with every outer yardarm flying a Royal Naval Ensign, and two large Ensigns flying from each mast – the largest from the main mast, just as we had 'down South' when we entered San Carlos. This wasn't normal protocol and we had to get permission from above to do so. The ship looked impressive. We even had our own Penguin mascot that we bought back with us in the form of CY George Mellor in his penguin suit, standing at the very front of the ship. The ship's company that were not involved with any seamanship were mustered on the flight deck and drilled to march to the port and starboard walkways, to line the sides as we sailed in.

The special day had arrived and I was to do a very special job. I was anchor 'Bunting' again, this time counting the cables back in. As soon as it was announced we were under way, the Jack came smartly down and was stowed into its bag in such a way that I knew, when the first line across was secured, the Union Flag would hoist up the

Jack Stay, smoothly and quickly unfurling to fly as the Union Jack, and we were home and secure!

We sailed towards the beach and Southsea, with a flotilla of small boats and our LCUs and LCVPs following in our wake, and what I saw took my breath away! All along the seafront were thousands of people, waving flags and cheering. We turned to Port to steer into the harbour entrance. I was on the Port side, but it didn't stop me turning my head to see what the crowds and noise were all about. There were almost 10 times as many people along the front, lining up to and past Billy Manning's funfair, all the way along the sea wall and the 'hot wall' as there had been 100 days ago, almost precisely to the hour, when we sailed south.

The Round Tower, a traditional base for waving goodbye to Sailors, was packed with hardly room to breathe. Prior to entering the Harbour mouth, the lads on the signal decks smartly pulled the extra Ensigns down and back to proper protocol. HMS Dolphin was fully lined with Sailors, WRENS and Civvies. As we sailed past the traditional piping salute was made, and then for the first time, we received a Cheer Ship from an establishment!

We sailed through the entrance to the Harbour and, as I looked out over towards Gosport, the crowds were equally as packed and enthusiastic. The blocks of flats were bedecked in Union flags, Ensigns, bunting and all kinds of banners. The Gosport Ferries were full to overload, and back on the other side at the Still and West (a popular local pub) more people and HMS Vernon, another Cheer Ship. The Hard as totally crowded! I was beside myself with joy and utter jubilation. I had such a lump in my throat and was holding back the tears, commenting and laughing and joking with the lads either side, trying not to get noticed by the Senior Rates on the fo'c'sle, who with joviality told us to wind our necks in and be smart!

As we sailed past Victory gate we came across a US Guided Missile destroyer, which was apparently on a pre-planned exercise and visit to Portsmouth. Hooters sounded as we passed each and every ship in the Dockyard and then it was often 2 or 3 tied alongside each other and every ship blared their sirens and cheered ship for us. This was crazy. It was out of this world. This was not what I expected; but God was it what we needed to tell us we were home, to tell us that we had done the right thing and the country wanted to thank us for all we had achieved, lost and sacrificed.

We sailed further up the harbour to turn to Starboard, and towards our berths at Fountain Lake Jetty (FLJ). We could hear the band playing as we turned the corner, and then the loudest cheers, as the families saw the ships for the first time! They didn't stop cheering and the ships along our way didn't stop with the sirens. I was blown away completely!

I looked around to see what the crowds were like, what number of people could possibly make such noise. There were thousands of people lining FLJ, with banners, all waving frantically at the ships. People were on the flat roofs of the Dockyard buildings and up cranes to get the best views. The band was playing keeping the crowds entertained, though I suspect at this point no one could hear them or had given up listening as we glided gracefully towards our berths and slipped gently alongside.

The Cable party were fallen out from Procedure Alpha, the rest of the ship's company had to remain along the walkways at attention. I've no idea, but I bet there wasn't many of them keeping strict discipline and not waving or chatting excitedly to their oppo next to them! I turned smartly right and forward to fall out and moved quickly to the Jack Staff.

I looked at the crowd briefly to see if I could see my Mum and Dad, first glance revealed nothing. As the bow edged closer to the dockside, I had the halyard in hand ready for the line being secured when, right in front of me, straight ahead was a wild and crazy woman, jumping, crying, waving like a lunatic and screaming my name. It was Tania! Behind her the rest of the family, a big banner proclaiming "Welcome Home Kayjers!" and there they were right smack bang in the middle of the bow, my family - my Mum and Dad, Tania and Michael, Andrew and Gary, the little Vangel, all waving excitedly, tears of joy and laughter streaming down their faces. I pointed and grinned the biggest grin a Cheshire Cat could ever grin, to let them know I'd seen them.

I hadn't lost sight of the line being hauled through the hawser by the Dockies, who had caught the monkey fisted piece of rope that was connected to the thick wire cable that was to connect us with home once and for all! I watched intently as the cable splashed into the water, the Fo'c'sle Officer leaning over the side to keep an eye on progress. I watched as the cable was hauled out of the water, and the loop was in the hands of a Dockyard worker. I watched as he roughly hauled it over the bollard, not taking my eyes of it, even though all I wanted to do was be shore-side and in the arms of my waiting family; and then he dropped the loop over the bollard and I shot the Union Jack up the Staff with such speed, it appeared to hardly move and it was there as if it had always been!

I hastily secured the halyards tightly so they didn't flutter in the wind; I undid the Jack Bag from the railings and then I turned and I waved at my family! I shouted at them that I had to go back to the bridge to secure and close down and I pointed up at the bridge wing to let them know where I would be. I would see them in a few minutes.

When I looked up and aft, the ship's company were waving like crazy; those on the Port side were all turning around. It seemed like an age, but the Order "Ship's Company, Diiisssmisss!" was broadcasted as loudly as the Chief GI could muster and with some style (not quite Sergeant Major, but good enough for a Matelot). There were shouts and cheers as everybody rushed to the Starboard waist to catch a glimpse of their loved ones for the first time. Everybody pointing and waving and shouting out as they found their wives, fiancées, Mums and Dads, their brothers and sisters, friends and, in my case, to my absolute shock, and joy - cousins!

Faz was there on the dockside with Mai, Lisa, Terry and Andrew standing behind my Mum and Dad! I suspected they were staying with him when they came down. They always did, and I'm sure their reunion was equally as emotional the night before; but to see him standing waiting on the Dockside greeting a warship home and safe after being sunk, losing all your possessions, your friends and nearly your own life, was a real mark of the man Chief Petty Officer Alan Fazackerly. I was dumbstruck and moved to tears by seeing him there. I really could not believe it!

I rushed up to the bridge, to help secure our area of the ship for leave. Whilst I was doing this with the team, I

FEARLESS - The Diary of an 18 Year Old at War in the Falklands

kept nipping to the wings to look down at the crowds. Everyone on the bridge wings was doing the same, even the officers and the Senior Rates. I don't think anybody could truly believe the force of the welcome that greeted us that day. There were literally thousands of people at FLJ, cheering, clapping, and singing with the band as it played with all the patriotic fervour it could muster.

We watched as the Skipper was the first down the Gangway, as was tradition, to greet his family and the 'Brass' that had come to greet the ship, as well as welcome our families to this reunion of all reunions.

At last we were secured, and leave was piped. Bill and I went down to the mess and I went down to get myself together before going ashore. It was pointless queueing just yet, and a couple of last minute muster of civvies that we were taking on leave, were a great distraction from the torrent of emotions I was experiencing.

I was ready, and with Bill, we made our way up to the forward gangway to finally step on dry land and be back in the arms of our families and safely home!

There was still a queue of Sailors, slowly moving down the gangway, being held up by the joyous hugs of Mums and Dads, wives and girlfriends and whoever else that could jump into the melee! I was just so very, very excited. I could see my family waving at me from the jetty. I gradually reached the end of the gangway and now it was my turn to be bowled over – almost literally. I must have had an even bigger smile on my face than I had on the foc's'le, as I walked quickly to my family who were moving at pace towards me. Tania was leading, running at me and grabbing me into her arms almost knocking me over, closely followed by my two little brothers Gary and Andrew, then Mum, then Dad. I was stuck in the middle of the greatest circle of love I have ever experienced. I couldn't breathe. I didn't want to breathe. I wanted to be crushed by this love and never let it go. Eventually, the crush subsided and individually I was welcomed by the happiest smiles and hugs from Dad, Mum, Tania, the boys and Stuart. Being only 3, he probably wasn't really sure what it was all about, but was happy to have been jumping up and down on Dad's shoulders, waving his flag and stabbing Dad in the cheek in the process, dressed in his little sailor's uniform, cheering and joining in with everything.

Faz made his way through and shook my hand and welcomed me home with his lopsided, cheeky grin. Mai, Lisa, Terry and Andrew also had their go. I was so pleased to see them all and proud that after all they had gone through that they had taken the time to come and welcome me home. I'm sure their experience was far more emotional than mine and I was overwhelmed to see them.

Whilst this was happening, Dad was cracking open the Champagne. He'd bought 3 bottles down with him. He popped the first cork, and it spouted its bubbles out over the jetty and over my hands as he passed me the bottle to take the first drink. And first drink I did! I nearly gulped down half the contents before the bubbles started coming back up through my nose, and I started coughing the contents out with everybody around me laughing and cheering at my idiocy and childish enthusiasm to be a man!

Once things had settled down, I found Bill and his and my parents reacquainted themselves again. I still remember Melanie, his sister, her tear-drenched cheeks and smile on her face, it really was a beautiful moment to add to a beautiful day!

We made our way briefly on board through the hordes to pick up my grip for the night. First I took the family up to the Bridge to show them our 'wounds', spinning the dit on how life on board at war had been. I probably terrified the life out of my poor Mum when I showed her how close the bullet hole was and the damage below to the Captain's cabin deck head. I pointed out where the rockets were found and how the 10" lantern had been and what happened when it took the hit, then it was back down through the crowds to the mess

The mess as tiny as it was, was crammed to the gunnels with families, the children tucked in to the 'Red Cross' parcels, the cans of Coke and goffas that were in the fridge. The adults drank McEwans Export 'Red Death' or Lager; as Junior Rates, we were not allowed wine or spirits in the mess, so the females had to make do with what we had. There was lots of joshing and jostling and laughter! I reached in the fridge to get some tinnies out for our two parties and handed across to Bill and his Dad and mine, Faz and Michael. We necked them in double quick time and got out of there to shore-side and safety! Bill only lived just outside Aldershot and was straight off home. We, on the other hand, had some catching up to do, and my Dad knew it was important for the lads to 'decompress' after active service and I decompressed in style!

First stop, the Ships Leopard and down into its cellar bar, or 'The Nut Bar', with everybody to have a drink 'away' from the crowds - it was packed! Bearing in mind, we had already shared 3 bottles of champagne, I'd had at least 2 tins of 'Red Death' and now some real beer in a real pub on solid ground with my Dad! This was the start of things to come for the next 3 or 4 months.

I managed to get a minute with Faz to spin some dits, which he wasn't really up for. I had to thank him for coming and acknowledged to him how hard it must have been to do this. With his usual nonchalance, he shrugged it off, and we got on with it! It was then that he told me how he had tried to contact me on the Fearless after landing on our deck. I couldn't believe what I was hearing, and my heart swelled with pride at knowing this man who still thought of others when his life was in peril and he had lost everything only minutes before.

I can honestly say, that I do not remember any more of this day!

45

Millom

What I do know, is that I was on duty that weekend, so could not go straight home. I was not uncomfortable with this as I knew I would be going home the following Thursday. As part of all the celebrations and adulation of the armed forces that year, Mac managed to obtain four buckshee tickets for the Royal Tournament! He wanted me to go with him and his fiancée at the time, "Oh and can you remember the picture of Debbie, Kev? She would like to meet you as well!" I couldn't remember saying I'd like to meet her but, at some point, I'm sure I'd made the right noises to Mac that his future bridesmaid was quite an attractive young lady who I wouldn't mind getting to know a lot better!

So there I was, the following Thursday afternoon on the Pompey to Waterloo train heading for my first blind date, when I could have been going home. The Royal Tournament was good fun, but I think my head was not in the right place for romance. All I could think of was getting home to Millom and catch up with friends and family. I knew Paula wasn't going to be there on the Friday as she had booked a holiday to Torquay with some mates. If I had gone up on Thursday, then that would have been different, which might have had something to do with my attitude at the time!

Mac and his party dropped me off at the Home Club in Waterloo and, after a rather awkward farewell with Debbie, I really wasn't that interested and she was not unattractive either, I hit the pit and tried to get my head down.

Sleep wouldn't come that easily. I flitted in and out, either because I was in a proper bed for the first time in months or the excitement of going home. I got up early and over to Euston for the long journey North. Dad asked me to wear my uniform home but at the time, even with all the love towards the armed forces, we were told not to wear them through London because of the IRA threat. My uniform was slung over my shoulder in a suit cover and I got on the train home.

"We'll pick you up at Ulverston." Dad said in my phone call home a day earlier.
"It's all right, I can get the connection to Millom."
"No" said Dad, "You'll have to change and wait around and I'm sure you'd rather get straight home!"
No point arguing the case!

With the usual supply of sandwiches and 'Red Death' I travelled up from Euston to Lancaster to change for Millom. The trains up there in those days were still the 50s/60s rolling stock and many of the carriages had individual compartments that you sat in, like the Hogwarts Express! I sat in mine with a couple of old ladies, sitting opposite each other chatting merrily away, while I supped more Red Death and anticipated what it would be like going back into the Cons victorious! The train pulled into Grange-Over-Sands and I waited for it to pull out again, so I could nip to the toilet to get changed into 'rig', as my Dad had requested. Ulverston was only 15 minutes or so away and I had to be ready.

I walked back into our compartment and the two ladies' faces were a picture! One said to the other "You didn't say your nephew was in the Navy!"
"He's not my nephew, lucky for me!" came the cheeky response.

I then explained where I had been and that I was now on my way home for the first time, which had them excited all over again and they both wanted to touch my 'dickie'! To the uninitiated and rude of mind, that's the blue collar on the uniform and it is supposed to bring any one who touches it good luck! Meanwhile, word got around that there was a sailor on the train who had just come back from the Falklands Conflict (not by mobile phone I might add, as they were not invented then!), and people were gathering outside the compartment. I was beginning to feel a little nervous and embarrassed by the attention. I prepared to leave the train, and the carriage passageway was full with everyone looking at me. I smiled nervously, and asked "Excuse Me" as I made my way along the carriage towards the door. They stepped aside and let me get closer to the door, with many pats on the back and well wishes.

As the train pulled up alongside the platform, I followed everybody off the train. I was nearer the front end of the platform and as I made my way through the crowded platform people were again staring at me. Finally, I saw my Dad, near the entrance, making his way towards me. I felt relieved to see him, so I could get out of the station and into the car, and away from the crowd. I was very conscious of the attention and feeling nervous. With Dad was an old school friend and close friend of the family, Dawn Myers. We'd known each other since I first moved up to Cumbria at 8 years old, as her Dad was in the Army and at Eskmeals with mine. It was brilliant to see her and she welcomed me back explaining she was driving me home.

I stepped out of the station to her waiting car – a yellow Mini. I loved it! I folded myself into the back seat and we set off. I tried to get out of Dad what sort of reception I'd get back in Millom. Something was obviously going on, but Dad wasn't letting on. Just a few friends and family waiting at home he said. I was still shocked at the reception I got on the train and on the platform and a little unnerved by it all.

Dawn got the three of us home as quickly as she could in her Mini, and as we came into Millom, she drove through the town centre and not Lancashire Road which was the quickest and easiest route to Market Street.

"Come on, tell me what's going on" I wanted to know, as we drove down Queen Street. "Nothing Son" he said with a smile on his face, and we turned the corner into Market Street.

The road had been closed off and I saw a crowd of people along the path, flags and bunting on the houses on both sides of the street and, hanging across the road, the White Ensign and a 'Welcome Home Kevin' banner, and a huge spread of food in the middle of the road.

I was overcome, and then Dawn pulled up right outside my house where my Mum was waiting with about 100 other people - family, friends and neighbours. I peeled myself out of the back seat and straight into my waiting

Mum's loving arms. It felt as good then as it did days before when I stepped off the gangway. There were loud cheers from everybody gathered outside the house.

A street party! This was some welcome. I really was stunned, speechless and struggled to keep my emotions in check. I just stood on the pavement looking around at everything and everyone, shaking my head, grinning, poking my tongue into my cheek, wiping my face, pointing at and acknowledging people, everybody was still clapping and watching me. I really could not speak. Tania bought me out a beer and I took a massive swig from the tin. It wasn't till that point, about 3 minutes after I arrived, that I could speak and actually move from the spot I was standing on. Suddenly, Britannia with her Trident appeared in the form of Mrs Foster, came bounding towards me and gave me a big hug! I was totally blown away and could not believe that people would do this for me.

The party was the brain child of Barbara Murning (Jonny's Mum), who got the neighbours galvanised into doing this. Many people chipped in to make it a success, baking, making banners and decorations, supplying food, and a fantastic fruit cake in the shape of a sailor's hat with the HMS Fearless cap tally around it.

My best mate Stuart Hartley was there, with others. Mr Guildford spent a couple of hours with us; this time we were able to have a better conversation about Mrs Thatcher and her Cabinet. The local press were there as well, taking photos, which initially was fine but they stayed on longer than was acceptable. I got upset with one of them, who kept trying to get an interview with me. Eventually Dad told them to leave. The other piece that was worrying me about the press is that other young men had died, and I felt really awful that parents would read about my celebrations. What did they have to celebrate?

For me, I really was shocked at the rapturous reception. It is difficult for many to believe but I was fairly shy at the time, all this attention, as brilliant as it was, made me feel uncomfortable. I fully understood the sentiment and loved the fact that my neighbours, friends, and even strangers, felt they wanted to do this but, deep in my mind, was a lot of noise of what had just gone past. I had frequent thoughts of those that didn't come back and found the constant questioning – not just on this day, but for many months later – by friends and children asking if I had killed anybody difficult. What was it like firing guns, seeing planes get blown up, and ships sinking? For all of these thoughts, and at some point later that night, my Mum tells me I spent about an hour on the stairs crying. I had consumed a lot of alcohol throughout the day, was emotionally drained, and finally I was safe and sound in my own home – still with many other people around. This must have been an outpouring of emotion for everything that had happened and I needed it. I would not have wanted it any other way and I still have a very strong sense of belonging to Millom and the people that supported me so much there. I am as proud of those people as I am for what we achieved down South. Without them life could have been so much more difficult.

The name of the book comes from my Dad's welcome home speech:

"Ladies and Gentlemen, I'd like to propose a toast, not necessarily to Kevin, I think he's done his bit, I think we

have all shown him that and I don't think it is necessary to raise a glass for a young man who's come back and certainly given ourselves as a nation our pride back, and certainly himself as a young man off for the first time to shot and shell; coming back successfully!

So I would like to propose two toasts. The first one to those unfortunate young men who were left behind in the Falkland Islands, who did their bit for us all, who unfortunately did not make it back. They're the chaps, who I think most thoughts are with during this sort of period. I would ask you ladies and gentlemen please, to raise your glass to 'The Fallen'!

And finally on a more HAPPY note…

Barbara Murning, when we decided we were going to have a bit of a beano for Kevin, she thought that this was not going to be the right and proper thing to do; and among the many, many, many other acts of kindness that we have had over this rather trying period from people such as yourselves, and as I said before total strangers in many cases, Barbara leapt forward and said we would like to put our faces forward. I thought how very, very nice of you. And she has done with all the good ladies that have helped her; and they have produced for us a super spread, they've knocked this young man flat on his back; he doesn't know if he is coming or going at this moment and I doubt if he will tomorrow lunchtime! Not if I have my way!

However I would ask you now please, or certainly my family rather than all the rest of you to raise a glass to Barbara and all her very, very, very willing band of helpers who have done so much to make this such a

*success for Kevin. SO TO EVERYONE WHO'S WORKED –
GOD BLESS YOU! THANK YOU BARBARA!*
*And would you like to go and enjoy it, because I'm
bloody well going to!"*

And enjoy it we bloody well did!

'Well that's the lot 'thank God' & now I can believe it's all
over, 'coz we're home. So here finally ends my diary of the
Falklands Crisis.'

It has taken me 12 years to get to this point from first
typing the original words into my computer. It has been a
torrid journey; an emotional turmoil with a lot of tears and
chuckles. Periods where I have not been able to put words
onto paper, leaving it for weeks on end before having the
courage to let the feelings free. Freeing those feelings
has un-blocked something in my mind; I feel rejuvenated,
clear, centred and focussed. It's easy to suggest I should
have done this years ago but it wasn't the right time then,
now is now, and it has worked in many ways.

I hope you have enjoyed my 'FEARLESS – The Diary of An
18 Year Old at War in The Falklands'

At the time, I did, I didn't and I did! I am grateful to the
many people who I fought alongside, those that took the
piss, laughed, taught, motivated, wrote to me, and sent
me gifts; this all got me through those manic months in
spring 1982. Even Tom Sawyer!

Epilogue

Half Naked Sailor Smashes Window

From the time we arrived back into Portsmouth to the time I finally left HMS Fearless in August 1983, I had one huge party!

The street party kicked it off, and as my Dad said, 'I didn't know what hit me.' The feeling was incredible; adulation, love, support, fun and laughter to tears, worries and anxieties; it had it all!

I partied hard that day, I didn't really have much choice. I didn't complain, I just got on with it and joined in the fun – it was all about me!

Dad could see at one point that I was beginning to flag, and took me off to the Conservative Club for a quiet beer and a chat.

"Hang on Dad, I'm just going to get changed."
"What for? Step out proud in your uniform son, you've earned the right."
"I'll be two minutes."
And I disappeared upstairs to change into my Chinese tailor made 'box' suit, that I designed in a very 1980's

fashion style and it was cut and sewn by 'Sew-Sew'.

I'm sure I was a disappointment to my Dad who had always been proud of his uniform and used to have to step out of barracks in it in his youth. Though being in the Kings Troop Royal Horse Artillery stepping out in full number ones, tight jodhpurs, braided jacket etc. was a damn sight more glamorous than a sailors uniform. However, to this day, I don't know why I didn't wear my uniform to go for that beer with my Dad. Perhaps I had had enough of the attention, though wearing a smart, hand tailored suit in Millom drew enough looks, and of course the world knew I was coming home that weekend. I believe he was really proud of me and what we had all achieved, and wanted me to be the same. I am, though at that moment in time I was probably feeling it.

I was informed a lot later, that at some point in the lateness of night/early morning I walked out of the party at home and sat half way up the stairs, just sobbing and crying my heart out. No one could console me, not even my Mum. In the end, my Dad told everyone to just leave me alone. Was this relief? Release? Or a portent of what was to come? I did something similar in a civilian psychiatrist's office 20 years later while explaining what I was going through, the memories I had, the fears and anxieties I was suffering from and how I wasn't coping. Then only to be told by him there was nothing wrong with me! Crying for 45 minutes in front of a complete stranger is probably not normal behaviour.

In September 1982, the ship was visiting Newcastle and back to South Shields where we had taken her out of refit only 1 year earlier. All sorts of events were arranged for the ships company including an invite by Lewis Collins to the Premier of the film 'Who Dares Wins'. I chose to go home to Millom!

I had gone out on the Saturday night to the usual haunts, drank a lot of beer with my Brother-in-Law Colin and we went on to one of the two clubs in Millom. I told Colin I would only go if I stopped drinking and we would only buy me orange juice and lemonade. This was a very rare occurrence indeed, but I had finally had enough.

This did happen, and I was merrily sipping away, meeting people who I hadn't seen since before I went to war all offering to buy me drinks, which I refused. However I found out several weeks later, that whilst I was away from the bar, some of my 'friends' felt they couldn't buy me soft drinks and thought it fun to top up my orange juice and lemonades with Vodka and white rums!

I do remember going home that night, Dad had cooked a curry, though when I was going to bed, I collapsed in a snotty heap on the landing and Dad had to help me the rest of the way to my bed.

The next thing I remember is coming to in a shed somewhere, naked from the waist down!

It was starting to get light outside, and I had no idea where I was or why I had no clothes on.

I looked around me to try to find my trousers and shoes but couldn't. I found a green plastic jacket hanging up in the shed, and I put that on to cover me and stepped out of the shed into a strange back yard.

When I went through the gate to the back street, I

realised I was in the next street up from Market Street, the Milkman was doing his rounds, and I casually walked passed and round the corner to get home. I climbed into my bed and fell asleep.

I had a niggling feeling throughout the day, that something had happened, though I could not remember what. And then just as I was about to go out for the evening there was a knock on the door; Detective Constable Colin Burroughs and a uniformed Police Sergeant were standing at the door, asking to speak to me.

They explained that they suspected I had broken a window and stolen a gardening jacket and a pair of boots. I was still confused. My Mum and Dad were in the lounge with me as the conversation was taking place and I still had no idea what had happened. The police went into my bedroom and there was the jacket in the corner.

I was arrested and taken down to the local Police station. My niches were still on the door frame where I used to go and get measured every month when I was 15 years old, to see if I had made the height of 5'7 3/4" so I could join the Police as a cadet. That was what I had wanted to do since I was about 5 years old, and join the mounted division. I did make the height, but the police never responded to my application form and the Royal Navy did!

They locked me in a cell and left me there for what seemed an eternity, then DC Borroughs took me into a room with the Sergeant and explained why I was there. He even made a suggestion that I had done this to get to the lady of the house as she was a very attractive woman. At this point I became scared that he was going to fit me up for something heinous, and I did start to become angry at such a suggestion. I was a sailor just back from war, in a small town. I had no end of offers and I certainly did not need to go and force myself on someone. I knew the family well, I went to school with her husband's sister and my brother was best friends with his brother. I asked for a solicitor and the DC told me I would have to be locked up until Monday if I started causing problems and there wouldn't be one available. I was now beginning to panic.

They produced a bag, with my clothing and shoes in it. My bright Chinese made boxer shorts, 16 pleat trousers and black suede winkle picker shoes. Apart from the fact no bloke in town would wear such outrageous clothing. Unfortunately, they were soiled. It was explained, that the Police Sergeant was ex - Royal Navy and he recognised the 'Dhoby Number' (a number allocated to you by the Chinese laundry), and as the only Sailor in town that weekend, it had to be me.

I explained to them that I had no idea what had happened. There was no recollection apart from waking up in the shed and walking home. I didn't even know a window had been broken.

The DC then explained that I had to write a statement and he would dictate to me to tell me what happened. If I did this, I could go home as soon as it was complete, otherwise I would be locked up for the weekend.

What choice did I have? I apologised profusely to the two officers for creating a problem for them and offered a suggestion that I go around to see the couple as I knew them, apologise and pay for any damage. The DC became aggressive and told me in no uncertain terms that if I went anywhere near the house or them, he would have me arrested and charged with witness intimidation. I was now very worried by the turn of events and agreed. To this day, I have still not apologised personally to the couple for my misdemeanour.

The statement was duly written, and I cannot remember if it was me that wrote it or not, but I did sign it. I was bailed to appear in Millom Magistrates Court on the Tuesday.

When I got out of that awful place and away from the equally awful bully that was DC Burroughs, my Dad wanted to know what had happened and sat me down to talk to me about the pressures of battle and the effects it can have. Siting this as incident an example. "You have to explain to your Solicitor that you have just returned from war. You believe you are suffering stress because of this. And you have to use this as a mitigating circumstance in court when you talk to the Magistrate."

I didn't. How could I tell the world, the town who believed me to be a hero, that I was suddenly struggling to cope. I was turning mental. What would they think of me? It was a small town, I would become the town 'looney'. I couldn't.

The outcome was: £25.00 fine for 1 count of criminal damage, £25.00 for 1 count of theft and £25.00 damages and compensation. And of course, a criminal record.

On return to HMS Fearless, I was also charged under the Naval Discipline Act and placed at the Captains table, where I received further punishment and the stinging words from Captain Larken "I do not need people like you on my ship."

I had let everybody down, me, my family, the townsfolk of Millom and now the Captain.

The story inside the local newspaper read "Half Naked Sailor Smashes Window". I'd gone from front page hero to villain and embarrassment in 3 months.

This was the start of my journey into 'sub-clinical' PTSD. As part of this I was also beginning to suffer from psoriasis on various parts of my body, and as the anxiety and depressions set in, this would become much worse, covering me from head to toe.

My wife would bear the brunt of my 'nihilistic personality' that had developed and live at times in despair with my anxiety and depression, and watch me destroy myself and eventually it took its toll on both of us and our marriage broke down after 30 years.

The Future

Once I left the Navy and settled into some sort of career, eventually in Human Resources gaining a Post Graduate Diploma in Personnel Management, I carved out a successful career working at a senior level on leadership teams. I chopped and changed jobs every 2 or 3 years, never settling.

I then discovered the power of Neuro Linguistic Programming (NLP). NLP helped me like nothing else had. I had years of CBT counselling and didn't really change. Graham Carter MM, did a 'sub - modalities change' intervention, which stopped me drinking red wine - I have not drunk red wine or port since my NLP Practioner

Course in 2014. He also gave me tools to manage my anxiety and emotions I was dealing with whilst writing this book. I would be typing on trains and planes whilst travelling with my role and come to certain points in the Diary where the memories were too painful, which would create tears streaming down my face in public. I would close the PC or laptop down and not return to it for months. He encouraged me to set goals and one of these goals was to complete my diary by 24th December 2014.

I had been writing this diary properly since 2008. I had written 20,000 words before September 2014. From that day with Graham, I completed my work with another 50,000 words between September and December 24th, 2014! I then qualified as an NLP Master Practitioner in 2015.

This was powerful stuff and I knew then what I wanted to do with my life - support others that what to make powerful and positive change. NLP can do this, it has happened with me, and I have helped others with issues to change and become successful.

I then qualified as a Professional Hypnotherapist achieving my diploma in March 2015 trained by Trevor Ramshaw HMS Exeter. Hypnotherapy is a world of Rapid Results Coaching for me. I have helped individuals alleviate pain and walk comfortably again. Helping people move on from traumas and abuse. Others have doubled their salaries or increased their business, and a stroke survivor who wasn't eating to eat again and find renewed physical strength to astound his physiotherapist with the rapid change in his movement and now mobility.

Smokers, stop smoking after 2 hours with me and people lose weight safely, effectively and maintain that weight loss.

My journey through PTSD to Hypnotherapy will be the next book that will be written to share my journey and help other people to understand that they do not have to suffer and there are ways in which them can make positive and lasting change.

Glossary of Jack Speak

3C1 Mess	Compartment where we lived and slept
4.5 Mag	Large shells magazine - see NGS
40/60	2nd World War anti-aircraft gun
AAC	Army Air Corp
Action snack	Food to keep us going - probably a pasty and an apple
Action/emergency stations	Ready for anything that might happen
Air Raid Warning Yellow	Enemy aircraft within 100 miles
Air Raid Warning Red	Enemy aircraft within 60 miles
Argy	Argentinian national
Bomb Alley	San Carlos Water – named by the press
Booties	Boot Necks or Royal Marines
Bridge	Where the Captain drives the ship
BTY	Battery - Unit of the Royal Artillery
Cable Flags	Numerical flags used to indicate length of anchor cable in the water
CAP	Combat Air Patrol - Sea Harriers
Captains Rounds	Cleanliness is next to Godliness - inspection of living and work areas to keep the ship sparkling
CCY	Communications Chief Yeoman
CDO	Commando
Colours	Daily ceremony of raising the White Ensign & Union Jack
Commanders Table	I'm in the shit!
Commodore Staff	Staff of a senior officer
Dhobi Wallers	Chinese Laundry men
Dit	Story/Exaggerated tale
DMS boots	Directly Moulded Sole - anti-static, anti-slip general issue Royal Navy boot
Docky's	Dock Yard workers
Earn the Queens shilling	Payment in days of old for being 'Press ganged' into the RN - usually dropped into a pint of ale and if an individual picked it out the bottom of his pot - he took the Queens shilling and was dragged on board

EOD	Explosive Ordnance Disposal - Very brave unit of the Army
Exocet	Lethal French missile
Fo'c'sle	Deck at the pointy end of the ship
GMD	Guided Missile Destroyer
GPMG	General Purpose Machine Gun
Grip	Holdall/Weekend bag
Hands to bathe	Relaxation by jumping of the ships side in the middle of the ocean. 'A marksman kept watch on the bridge wing in case of sharks; if he saw any he would shout a warning then shoot the person furthest away from the ship.'
Jack Blair	Royal Navy Tailor/Shop of dubious clothing
Joss	The 'Boss' ships policeman
Killick Reg	Ships Policeman
Leave watch	Duty for those left behind whilst rest of ship's company are on holiday
LCU	Landing Craft Utility
LCVP	Landing Craft Vehicle Personell
LMG	Light Machine Gun
LSL	Landing Ship Logistical
Maily	Letter
Matelot	Sailor – mid-19th century slang, derived from the French word matenot
MCO	Main Communication Office
Mine Warfare	Specialist division of the Royal Navy
MUPPET	Most Useless Person Pusser Ever Trained – usually a not very bright or skilled individual
NGS	Naval Gunfire Support - big bangs and headaches for the enemy
On watch	Shift work
OOW	Officer of the Watch
Pot mess	Stew with everything thrown in
Port side	Left hand side of the ship
Procedure Alpha	Dress in best uniform to look smart when leaving harbour

Rapier	Land-based surface to air missile system
RAS	Replenishment at sea – see RFA
RFA	Royal Fleet Auxiliary – best supply ships in the world
Rig nos 1s	Best uniform
Russian AGI.	Auxiliary Gathering Intelligence – thinly disguised as a Trawler with far too many aerials
SAS, SBS & Booties	Very hard and skilled fighting men
SBS Chatham	Stand By Squadron - not Special Boat Service - though it always sounded impressive when you were 17!
Scran	Food
SCYO	Senior Communications Yeoman's Office
Sea Cat	1960s old and slow ships surface to air missile system
Sea Dart	Long-range and brilliant surface to air missile
Sea Wolf	Excellent close in weapon system against aircraft- when it worked!
SHAR	Sea Harrier Air Reconnaissance
Signal deck	Place of work with flashing lights and flags
SLR	Self Loading Rifle
Sprog	Young sailor
Stbd side	Right hand side of the ship
STUFT	Ships Taken Up From Trade - Requisitioned Merchant ships
TEZ	Total Exclusion Zone - we'll sink you if you enter!
TF	Task Force A scary sight of large numbers of ships – "The Government have now decided that a large Task Force will sail as soon as all preparations are complete." Margaret Thatcher 1982
TG	Task Group - Group of ships/ units for specific operations e.g. Amphibious Task Group
TU	Task Unit Smaller groups of Ships/ units

CTF	Commander Task Force - Most senior
CTG	Commander Task Group
CTU	Commander Task Unit
Tins	Tins of beer
Tot	Issue of rum
Trapped	Met a young lady
Turned to	Working
Up top	On the upper deck of the ship
UXB	Unexploded Bomb
Yardarms	Where the flag signals fly from high on the ships mast – and I hated climbing!

Argentine Aircraft Lost

Source:
http://www.naval-history.net/F64-Falklands-Argentine_aircraft_lost.htm

Information from Naval History website, to show comparisons from my information to that of 'official' information.

Saturday 3rd April
[a1] - Puma SA.330L of CAB 601 shot down at Grytviken, South Georgia by Royal Marine small arms fire.

Saturday 1st May
[a2, a3, a4] - One Pucara of FAA Grupo 3 destroyed and two more damaged and not repaired at Goose Green by CBUs dropped in attack by No.800 Sea Harriers flown by Lt Cmdr Frederiksen, Lt Hale and Lt McHarg RN (8.25 am). Lt Jukic killed in the destroyed aircraft.
[a5] - Mirage IIIEA of FAA Grupo 8 shot down north of West Falkland by Flt Lt Barton RAF in No.801 Sea Harrier using Sidewinder (4.10 pm). Lt Perona ejected safely.
[a6] - Mirage IIIEA of FAA Grupo 8 damaged in same incident north of West Falkland by Lt Thomas RN in No.801 Sea Harrier using Sidewinder. Then shot down over Stanley by own AA defences (4.15 pm) and Capt Cuerva killed
[a7] - Dagger A of FAA Grupo 6 shot down over East Falkland by Flt Lt Penfold RAF in No.800 Sea Harrier using Sidewinder (4.40 pm). Lt Ardiles killed.
[a8] - Canberra B.62 of FAA Grupo 2 shot down north of Falklands by Lt Curtiss RN in No.801 Sea Harrier using Sidewinder (5.45 pm). Lt Ibanez and Gonzalez ejected but are not rescued.

Sunday 2nd May
[a9] - Lynx HAS.23 of CANA 1 Esc embarked on ARA Santisima Trinidad lost in flying accident probably to north of Falklands.
[a10] - Alouette III of CANA 1 Esc lost on board ARA General Belgrano when she was torpedoed and sunk to south-west of Falklands.

Monday 3rd May
[a11] - Aermacchi MB-339A of CANA 1 Esc crashed into ground near Stanley approaching airfield in bad weather (4.00 pm). Lt Benitez killed.
[a12] - Skyvan of PNA damaged by naval gunfire at Stanley on the night of 3rd/4th and not repaired.

Sunday 9th May

[a13, a14] - Two A-4C Skyhawks of FAA Grupo 4 lost. Possibly damaged by Sea Darts from HMS Coventry or crashed in bad weather, with one aircraft found on South Jason Island. Lt Casco and Lt Farias killed.

[a15] - Puma SA.330L of CAB 601 shot down over Choiseul Sound by Sea Dart fired by HMS Coventry (4.10 pm). Crew of three lost.

Wednesday 12th May

[a16, a17, a18] - Two A-4B Skyhawks of FAA Grupo 5 shot down off Stanley by Sea Wolf fired by HMS Brilliant and third aircraft hit sea trying to evade missile (1.45 pm). All three pilots, Lt Bustos, Lt Ibarlucea and Lt Nivoli killed.

[a19] - A-4B Skyhawk of FAA Grupo 5 shot down over Goose Green by own AA fire (2.25 pm). Lt Gavazzi killed.

Saturday 15th May

[a20-a25] - Six Pucaras of FAA Grupo 3; [a26-a29] - Four T-34C Mentors of CANA 4 Esc; [a30] - Skyvan of PNA, all destroyed or put out of action at Pebble Island in raid by D Sqdn SAS (early morning)

Friday 21st May

[a31] - Chinook CH-47C of CAB 601 destroyed on ground near Mount Kent by Flt Lt Hare RAF in 1(F) Sqdn Harrier GR.3 using 30mm cannon (8.00 am).

[a32] - Puma SA.330L of CAB 601 badly damaged on ground near Mount Kent in same attack by Sqdn Ldr Pook and Flt Lt Hare RAF in 1(F) Sqdn Harrier GR.3s using 30mm cannon (8.00 am). Destroyed on 26th in same position by Sqdn Ldr Pook using CBUs.

[a33] - Pucara of FAA Grupo 3 shot down over Sussex Mountains by Stinger SAM fired by D Sqdn SAS (10.00 am). Capt Benitz ejected safely.

[a34] - Dagger A of FAA Grupo 6 shot down near Fanning Head by Sea Cat fired by HMS Argonaut or Plymouth, or more likely Sea Wolf from HMS Broadsword (10.30 am). Lt Bean killed.

[a35] - Pucara of FAA Grupo 3 shot down near Darwin by Cmdr Ward RN in one of three Sea Harriers of No.801 NAS using 30mm cannon (12.10 pm). Major Tomba ejected.

[a36, a37] - Two A-4C Skyhawks of FAA Grupo 4 shot down near Chartres, West Falkland by Lt Cmdr Blissett and Lt Cmdr Thomas RN in No.800 Sea Harriers using Sidewinders (1.05 pm). Lt Lopez and Lt Manzotti killed.

[a38] - Dagger A of FAA Grupo 6 shot down near Teal River Inlet, West Falkland by Lt Cmdr Frederiksen RN in No.800 Sea Harrier using

Sidewinder (2.35 pm). Lt Luna ejected.

[a39, a40, a41] - Two Dagger A's of FAA Grupo 6 shot down north of Port Howard, West Falkland by Lt Thomas and a third by Cmdr Ward RN in No.801 Sea Harriers using Sidewinders (2.50 pm). Maj Piuma, Capt Donaldille and Lt Senn all ejected.

[a42] - A-4Q Skyhawk of CANA 3 Esc shot down near Swan Island in Falkland Sound by Lt Morell RN in No.800 Sea Harrier using Sidewinder (3.12 pm). Lt Cmdr Philippi ejected.

[a43] - A-4Q Skyhawk of CANA 3 Esc also shot down near Swan Island in Falkland Sound in same incident by Flt Lt Leeming RAF in No.800 Sea Harrier using 30mm cannon (3.12 pm). Lt Marquez was killed.

[a44] - A-4Q Skyhawk of CANA 3 Esc damaged over Falkland Sound by small arms fire from HMS Ardent and again in same incident as above by Lt Morrell using 30mm cannon. Unable to land at Stanley with undercarriage problems and Lt Arca ejected (3.30 pm).

Sunday 23rd May

[a45] - Puma SA.330L of CAB 601 flew into ground near Shag Cove House, West Falkland attempting to evade Flt Lt Morgan RAF in No.800 NAS Sea Harrier (10.30 am). All crew escaped.

[a46] - Agusta A-109A of CAB 601 in same incident near Shag Cove House, West Falkland destroyed on ground by Flt Lt Morgan and Flt Lt Leeming RAF in No.800 NAS Sea Harriers using 30mm cannon (10.30 am).

[a47] - Puma SA.330L of CAB 601 also in same incident near Shag Cove House, West Falkland damaged on ground by Flt Lt Morgan with 30mm cannon (10.30 am). Then believed shortly destroyed by Lt Cmdr Gedge and Lt Cmdr Braithwaite RN in No.801 Sea Harriers with more cannon fire.

[a48] - A-4B Skyhawk of FAA Grupo 5 shot down over San Carlos Water by unknown SAM (1.50 pm). Claims that day include "Broadsword" Sea Wolf, "Antelope" Sea Cat, and land-based Rapiers and Blowpipe. Lt Guadagnini killed.

[a49] - Dagger A of FAA Grupo 6 shot down over Pebble Island by Lt Hale RN in No.800 Sea Harrier using Sidewinder (4.00 pm). Lt Volponi killed.

Monday 24th May

[a50, a51, a52] - Two Dagger A's of FAA Grupo 6 shot down north of Pebble Island by Lt Cmdr Auld and a third by Lt D Smith in No.800 Sea Harriers using Sidewinder (11.15 am). Maj Puga and Capt Diaz ejected, but Lt Castillo killed.

[a53] - A-4C Skyhawk of FAA Grupo 4 damaged over San Carlos Water

by ship and ground-based air defences and crashed into King George Bay, West Falkland on flight home (1.30 pm). Claims that day include "Argonaut" and "Fearless" Sea Cat, and Rapier and Blowpipe SAMs. Lt Bono lost.

Tuesday 25th May

[a54] - A-4B Skyhawk of FAA Grupo 5 shot down north of Pebble Island by Sea Dart fired by HMS Coventry (9.30 am). Lt Palaver killed.
[a55] - A-4C Skyhawk of FAA Grupo 4 destroyed over San Carlos Water by a variety of weapons, claims including small arms fire, "Yarmouth" Sea Cat, and Rapier and Blowpipe SAMs (12.30 pm). Lt Lucero ejected.
[a56] - A-4C Skyhawk of FAA Grupo 4 damaged over San Carlos Water in same attack, and then brought down north-east of Pebble Island by Sea Dart fired by HMS Coventry (12.45 am). Lt Garcia killed.

Thursday 27th May

[a57] - A-4B Skyhawk of FAA Grupo 5 damaged over San Carlos Water by 40mm Bofors from HMS Fearless or Intrepid, and crashed near Port Howard (5.00 pm). Lt Velasco ejected.

Friday 28th May

[a58] - Pucara of FAA Grupo 3 crashed into high ground between Goose Green and Stanley returning from attack in Goose Green area (c10.00 am). Lt Giminez killed.
[a59] - Aermacchi MB-339A of CANA 1 Esc shot down at Goose Green by Blowpipe SAM fired by Royal Marine Air Defence Troop (5.00 pm). Lt Miguel killed.
[a60] - Pucara of FAA Grupo 3 shot down at Goose Green by small arms fire from 2 Para (5.10 pm). Lt Cruzado ejected and became POW.

Saturday 29th May

[a61] - Dagger A of FAA Grupo 6 shot down over San Carlos Water by Rapier SAM (12.00 pm). Lt Bernhardt killed.

Sunday 30th May

[a62] - Puma SA.330L of CAB 601 lost in the morning in uncertain circumstances near Mount Kent, possibly to own forces fire.
[a63, a64] - Two A-4C Skyhawks of FAA Grupo 4 shot down east of Falklands by Sea Darts fired by HMS Exeter, although 4.5 inch gunfire from HMS Avenger may have hit one (2.35 pm). Lt Vazquez and Lt Castillo killed.

Tuesday 1st June

[a65] - Hercules C.130E of FAA Transport Grupo 1 shot down 50 miles North of Pebble Island by Cmdr Ward RN in No.801 Sea Harrier using Sidewinder and 30mm cannon (10.45 am). Crew of seven killed.

Monday 7th June

[a66] - Learjet 35A of FAA Photo-Reconnaissance Grupo 1 shot down over Pebble Island by Sea Dart fired by HMS Exeter (9.05 am). Wing Cmdr de la Colina and crew of four killed.

Tuesday 8th June

[a67, a68, a69] - Two A-4B Skyhawks of FAA Grupo 5 shot down over Choiseul Sound by Flt Lt Morgan RAF and a third by Lt D Smith in No.800 NAS Sea Harriers using Sidewinders (4.45 pm). Lt Arraras, Lt Bolzan and Ensign Vazquez killed.

Sunday 13th June

[a70] - Canberra B.62 of FAA Grupo 2 shot down west of Stanley by Sea Dart fired by HMS Exeter (10.55 pm). Pilot, Capt Pastran ejected safely but Capt Casado is killed.

Postwar - Captured at Stanley

[a71-a81] - Eleven Pucaras of FAA Grupo 3

[a82-a83] - Two Bell 212s of FAA Grupo 7

[a84-a86] - Three Aermacchi MB-339As of CANA 1 Esc

[a87] - Puma SA.330L of PNA

[a88] - Chinook CH-47C of CAB 601

[a89-a90] - Two Agusta A-109A Hirundos of CAB 601

[a91-a99] - Nine Iroquois UH-1Hs of CAB 601

Unknown Date

[a100] - Pucara of FAA Grupo 4 reported lost over in the Atlantic on reconnaissance mission from Comodoro Rivadavia.

Dad
In Memory of WOII P.J.A. Porter 1937 - 2010

Made in the USA
Columbia, SC
14 May 2017